Making *Limonada*

Making *Limonada*

Memories of an Andalucian Village
During the Last Years of Franco's Fascist Spain

Diana Cohen

DonaQuijote Press
San Francisco, California

MAKING LIMONADA

ISBN 978-0-9831509-0-9.
DoñaQuijote Press
www.donaquijote.com

Contributors

Cover Art – Girl on Beach, 1995 (watercolour on paper) by Lincoln Seligman, Private Collection/The Bridgeman Art Library, London
Photographs – By the author unless otherwise noted
Book Interior Design: Jim Bisakowski
Cover Design: Philip Noyes

By Diana Cohen

Earlier versions of *Summer in Sinai,* and *Rejoneadora,* were published in Best Women's Travel Writing, 2007 and 2008.

Bread, Clay and the Spanish Civil War, won Travelers' Tales 2009 Solas Awards Gold for Most Unforgettable Character.

In Memory of Pepe Cano Cortez,
Carmela Fernández Cruz and Paco Ramos
Enriquez, who trusted me with their stories
and opened their hearts, their families
and their lives to me.

Acknowledgements

Special thanks to my editor, Larry Habegger, whose wisdom and good counsel never led me or my stories astray. To Mary Tolaro Noyes and Tom Noyes, I am grateful for your many hours of hard work and unending support in seeing this book to completion. I deeply appreciate all the time my husband, Jerry Robinson, devoted to reading and editing my manuscript. He has encouraged me always. Loli Gamez Enriquez of San Francisco, who grew up in the village of Coín, 15 km from Fuengirola, has been a great help to me with the Andalucian dialect. So too has Verónica Riera Fernández of Asturias and Madrid, who spent two weeks living with us in San Francisco and gave me a remarkable gift: Through her eyes I fell freshly in love with my own country and came to understand in a new way why so many foreigners love America. Across the years I have been the beneficiary of many people's loving support: as a writer, a student, as a person and a parent: The late Percy and Alice Seitlin. (Percy gave me my first copy of *The Elements of Style*, and wished that it would mean as much to me as it did to him. It has indeed.) Professor Judith Berlowitz introduced me to Cervantes' Don Quijote at Mills College; she sagely never questioned my unwillingness to finish the last chapter. I think she understood my need for the noble dreamer, Don Quijote, to continue his adventures and live on within me. The late Rainer Mengleberg of Torremolinos, Antonio Villatoro, Patzi Haslimann, Janet Mendel of Mijas… they have all been generous and loving friends. I will always regard Narin Rasmussen and Sally Lindover as angels who appeared in my life when I needed an angel most. Dr. Marty Greenberg gave me useful advice on confronting writers' block: "Keep the seat of the pants on the seat of the chair."

The friendship and laughter that I have shared for more than forty years with Ann Karren Gitlis means we have become each other's historians. One could not ask for a more wonderful and generous hearted friend.

Having kept journals over the years my memories have been aided by frequent reference to their pages. Nonetheless these are my memories and my recollections of how things were. Someone else may of course have a different perspective on that time and place but that would be a different story. This is solely mine and all errors and mischaracterizations are my responsibility as well.

VALE

About the Author

Diana Cohen grew up among the oaks and sunburnt hills of Marin County, California. She lived for many years in *Andalucía*, Spain where she raised her four children. She also worked as a potter, taught English to Spanish students and trained as a *rejoneadora*, the artful bullfight from horseback.

After returning to California, Diana graduated from Mills College, where an inspired professor introduced her to Cervantes's *El Ingenioso Hidalgo Don Quijote de la Mancha*. After graduation she was a recipient of a Coro Fellowship in Public Affairs. She celebrated the four hundred year publication of Don Quijote by studying the novel in the city of Cervantes birth—Alcala de Heneres, Spain.

Across the years her adventures have continued by dory or kayak, by bicycle, with a backpack or a walking stick: Grand Canyon, Canyon de Chelley, Cuba, Machu Picchu, Zimbabwe, Turkey, and always devotedly back to Spain. For as the Greek Poet Cavafy said in *Ithica*: "Without her you would never have taken the road." She resides with her husband, Jerry Robinson, in San Francisco.

Contents

Prologue

If you love something hotly enough, consciously, with care, it becomes yours by symbiosis, irrevocably.

—Jan Morris

The humble, whitewashed fishermen's cottages were my first glimpse of the village as my three young children and I were driven in from the Rock of Gibraltar long ago. It was spring, 1964. Those one-story cottages lined the seafront and made Fuengirola—the small town that would become our home—a mere freckle on the map of southern Spain. Years later the cottages were bulldozed into chunks of rubble. On their graves rose tall, angular apartment blocks, seven and eight stories high, as alike as paper cut-outs, each with its wrought-iron balcony and view of the Mediterranean that feels like you can see into forever. These concrete blocks have brought untold prosperity to the children and grandchildren of the men and women who were born in those cottages, lived life on their doorsteps and died in their tiny dark rooms.

When we first arrived the empty beach on either side of town stretched on for miles. Now as far as the eye can see, monumental cranes and iron rebar jut into the sky, littering the coastline like skeletons of decaying mastodons. To my eyes it seems as though every soulless block of flats, every public space is made of marble, cold and unforgiving. The incessant rat-a-tat-tat of jackhammers assaults the air, ears and brain.

I like to think that the children and I were blown in on the waves after crossing the Atlantic on an old Italian liner. Despite the intervening years, my memories of this town, the people who lived here and the way it looked when we first knew it, remain vivid. I remember how each spring those fishermen's cottages were given a fresh coat of whitewash by old widows swathed in black. Until, over the decades, their surfaces ceased to have smooth, crisp angles and instead took on a crinkled and folded look, much like the faces of the tiny women who so proudly tended them.

What was it exactly that caused me to fall in love with this place so long ago? When we first arrived I was alone with my three children, unconsciously searching for a place to hide from memories and loss, hungry for a place to call home. What I couldn't have guessed was that Spain was the perfect place for hiding secrets, hiding as it was from its own painful past, the shame and horror of its Civil War (1936-1939) and the terrible years of reprisals and executions that followed. Death was like a fine dust that had settled on nearly every family, including mine. Spain and I fit each other perfectly.

We came and stayed awhile, then left for a time. Yet back we came again. And that's how it's been all these years. The next time I returned I brought a new husband—a father for my children. And now we had another little girl, just over the threshold of babyhood. What was the seduction? Was it the pace of village life and the people who became our friends? Was it all the animals that became a part of our family? Was my youthful self particularly susceptible to the allure of Andalucía? Or was it an artificial construct of my imagination, a sense of belonging and a chance to start my life anew?

Whatever it was and whatever it remains, I feel certain that the places we love reveal a key to our inner workings. Perhaps I'm writing this story to decipher that key. For something powerful keeps tugging me back here almost every year after the children and I finally sailed away from the Port of Málaga in the summer of 1976. It's most often in springtime that back I come like a salmon migrating home. A few days ago I arrived again at Málaga airport just before sunset, when the light was golden, as soft as the sweet, moist kiss of a child. It's always the same: I step off the plane and the intense pleasure of coming home makes me choke with tears. Yet the truth is it wasn't ever really our town…it just seemed that way after living here for so long at such an important time in our young lives. But then, what does truth have to do with the truths of the heart? For those years she was our town and I loved her. And I am one of her historians, or at least a historian of some of the events, a way of life and a few of her people. It was a simpler time that was incredibly sweet, and now is gone forever. So if I fail to tell her stories—Pepe's stories—as he told them to me, and my stories, as I lived them, who will be left to tell them?

In those years when my children and I were young, the beach was wide, the color of expensive pearls, and we could step outside our gate and dig our toes into the warm sand. Now there is a tiled promenade, the Paseo Marítimo, Principe de España, and a busy two-lane road that stretches from one end of town to the other. That promenade swallowed a good portion of the beach's girth. I love remembering it as I first knew it, when I would take the children by the hands and walk with them into the sea and the power of the waves would wash us up on the sand like so many lovely shells. The Mediterranean still laps languidly in the long, hot months of summer, but to my eyes what remains of the shore is merely a damp hemline.

The streets I walked as a very young woman have changed so much that now I'm forced to make my way around by Braille. Adding to my confusion, in the early years of Spain's *transición* to democracy, in an act of collective amnesia, the old street names were changed. Our old street, Calle José Antonio and Avenida Calvo Sotelo for example, were renamed to erase any reminders of *el Caudillo,* supreme leader General Francisco Franco and his fascist *Falange*—as if a name change could wipe from memory the nightmare of the Spanish Civil War. Even walking these streets which I'd walked a thousand times it is still hard for me to tell what was where. It's like a drawing on a child's tablet: the transparent top sheet has been lifted and what once was is now indistinct, barely imaginable.

Growing up here in Andalucía during Franco's tightly controlled regime was, like everything, both good and bad. During his thirty-seven years of rigid dictatorship, Spain was a country of social stability and security, at least on the surface. Children could walk alone to school and play in the streets until late on balmy summer nights. Young women like me could walk anywhere, accosted only by wolf whistles and hissed *piropos* like *¡guapa!* pretty! A darker side of the Franco years was a reality we lived with—anyone could anonymously make a *denuncia*—accusing anyone of anything to the hated Guardía Civil, the local symbol of Francoist repression. I'm sure I wasn't alone in always carrying the tiniest lurking fear that I or one of my children could disappear forever into their sinister ochre building with the inscription *Todo Por la Patria*—Everything for the Fatherland—chiseled over the lintel in big block letters. During those constrained years we lived in a surveillance society—neighbors spied on each other and us. Ears were listening everywhere. In spite of the sweetness and simplicity of village life there was an underlying sense of unease and a constraint on personal expression and behavior. It seems hard to imagine but couples couldn't embrace or kiss in public without worrying that they'd be denounced or arrested. But like the rest of the town's residents, we were all in it together; it certainly kept us honest and the village crime free. The Guardía Civil wielded absolute power in those years. When they passed along the streets, always in twos, with their cinched wide leather belts, thick pistols shoved deep into leather holsters, black patent leather hats curved against their foreheads in front with wings at the back, and olive green uniforms, I can remember feeling fear ripple through the streets like a sound-wave. Their stony faces and somber presence are gone now from the cities and towns, redirected to patrolling the highways and frontiers of the country.

Also gone forever from these narrow streets are the small details that made them feel like home to me: Tiny kitchens behind wrought-iron grills where by 2 o'clock the fruity scent of garlic frying in olive oil would float out seductively and make me swoon with hunger as I hurried home from the pottery or the stables to my own kitchen. Or the crackling sounds of fish frying and shellfish sizzling, and always the smell of olive oil and grilled bread and a thousand other aromas of our small town preparing to sit down to lunch. Today the streets are lined with steak houses, pizza joints and English pubs with bold signs proclaiming "*Menú del Día*— Bangers, Eggs and 2 Veg!" On the beachfront the odor of fish and chips and McDonald's burgers has overwhelmed the fragrance of open fires and sardines grilling slowly on wooden sticks over the coals, tended by young boys with their pants rolled up, barefoot on the sand.

Long gone is the central *mercado*—the morning market at the end of our street—with its lighthearted banter and the good-humored pandemonium of the women shopping for the fresh food we'd eat that day. The old fishermen wore jaunty caps and knee-high, black rubber boots with their pants stuffed inside. They had bristled whiskers and shrimp-pink swollen knuckles. I can still hear the voices of the brothers, Salvador and Pepe. "*¡Hay pescado fresco! señora*, nice fresh fish today," they would sing out merrily to me, and with a wink and a nod slip a fresh sardine to my white Pekin duck, Hurdy Gurdy, who had waddled his way behind me to market. They always acted as though giving him a few samples was just the way you treated any good customer. Now the brothers' weather-beaten faces have been replaced by serious men and women who sell fish as a business at the new market on the busy main road.

The brightly-painted fishing boats, hand-crafted by men who could neither read nor write, no longer lie tilted on the sand. I used to lie in bed at night listening to the lub-lub cadence of their motors thumping out a reassuring heartbeat to the sleeping town. The mantels of their oil lamps that cast magnesium-white ribbons of light on the ebony water and drew myriad species of fish to their nets, were long ago blown out.

The bar across the street, Los Hermanos, where Pepe the Potter would invite me for a mid-morning *café con leche* that we drank from tall glasses while standing at the bar with one foot resting on a brass rail below, closed its doors long ago. It was there that Pepe introduced me to *anise*, his daily dose of licorice-flavored firewater that he downed in one gulp; he swore it kept his pipes from corroding. And over there, on the opposite corner, is where on Sunday mornings the *churro* man had his big vat of bubbling oil set up in the street. I used to watch the curls of fried dough swim about in the foam. If the night before I had drunk too much Tio Pepe and my head ached, I'd order a pale yellow *manzanilla* tea from the bar inside and sip it while I waited for the *churros* I'd carry home for my family. Now all this activity has been shuttered and plastered over and even the echoes of the early morning din have been hushed and sent packing.

As I stroll along I can still see the occasional small, red-tiled roof of a fisherman's cottage wedged between eight- or even ten-story behemoths. From my beloved friend Carmela's balcony I can see the graceful curve of terracotta roof-tiles that form a line as curvaceous as a flamenco dancer's fingers. Behind the cottage is a tiny patio where an old *nispero* tree, a loquat, is laden with bright orange fruit in an act of faith for its future. Next to it a strapping fig tree with huge leaves the size of a giant's palm, is growing lustily, like a gangling adolescent. Next door—its towering neighbor all sharp lines and exact angles—sports a big television reception disk and doesn't even have balconies to soften its hard edges. How long the owners will resist demolishing this tiny house is anyone's guess. I root for these holdouts for they remind me that what I once knew and loved was not just a dream. But these small cottages are not long for this town no matter how softly and beguilingly the moss and algae grow on their roofs.

Retracing my steps of long ago I can hear vaguely familiar sounds ahead of me, like a giant beehive humming. It takes me a moment to recognize the high pitched shrieks of girls' voices bouncing off the thick walls of María Auxiliadora, my youngest daughter Lauren's first school. It's moved to the next block now, but it's still only a short walk from where our old house stood in all her whitewashed dignity. Lauren used to skip alone to school each morning in her blue-and-white checked pleated skirt and white blouse. How the nuns loved their smart little rosy-cheeked "Lorena!"

In those years I fancied myself quite Spanish and tried to cook like Pepe's wife, Carmela. The tiny rainbow-shelled clams called *coquinas* were one of our favorite lunchtime treats. I would sauté them briefly in olive oil, garlic and a splash of white wine until their shells popped open, then I'd rush them to our big wooden table in the patio, their shells still tap-dancing in the iron skillet. Malcolm and the children and I would inhale their fragrance and jostle each other for the best position to sop up their juices with crusty bread. I always thought I could almost hear the symphonic slurp of whole streets sucking in their meltingly sweet ambrosia. The bounty of the Mediterranean that was once amazing in its abundance and diversity is now meager, with much of the fish farm-raised to meet the appetites of a public who still loves its *pescado*.

I remember, too, the sputtering sounds of motorbikes reverberating off the stucco walls of our street and the sight of young women riding sidesaddle behind their *novios*—their boyfriends—one of her arms looped tightly around his waist.

Sometimes a whole family would be glued tightly together as the father wobbled his motorbike slowly through the streets. Almost no one owned a car in those days; democracy and prosperity had yet to come to southern Spain. Now these narrow streets, designed for bicycles and women carrying baskets, are choked with large cars. Carmela's son-in-law, Paco Verdun, the lawyer, brought us back to town yesterday after an excursion down the coast to Marbella where we sat beside the sea, talked and drank afternoon coffee while the children ran about. Leisure time in Spain is still all about family. Paco's black BMW SUV barely made the narrow turns. He'd back up and crank the wheel, moving forward in tiny fits and starts—like a portly woman struggling into a girdle—as he navigated his way through one-way streets that dead-ended in the detritus of yet more construction.

Instead of jackhammers I like to recall the sounds of the *zambomberos* and the tambourines and carolers at Christmas. The *zambomba*, a ceramic drum was shaped a bit like a flowerpot with a skin stretched tightly across one end and a stick stuck through its middle. You made a thumping, sobbing sort of noise by rubbing your spit-dampened hand vigorously up and down the stick. The first time we heard it we were all standing upstairs in our old dowager house with its big floor-to-ceiling windows thrown open to the cold night air, as the singers and *zambomberos* made their way down our street. Lauren, who was three, got really scared by its otherworldly sound, as only little children who are not yet accustomed to the world's surprises can be. I'll bet it's hard to find a *zambomba* now, but what wouldn't I give to hear that haunting hollow thump coming down the street again.

I recall too the somewhat discordant music of the O.J.E., the Organización Juvenil Española, a rag-tag but proud band of adolescents, horns blaring and drums thumping, marching down the street past our house. We would run out and stand in the open doorway to watch them, fascinated by a young bugle player with one leg many inches shorter than the other, who limped along keeping perfect pace with the martial beat.

After torrid summer days, it seemed like the whole town turned out to walk a *paseo* along the seafront in the soft night air. On Saturday and Sunday nights everyone dressed up and strolled arm-in-arm, pushing babies in their carriages. On many warm evenings like tonight, our family, ambling along licking ice cream cones, would meet Pepe and Carmela taking in the cool air, his arm draped affectionately about her shoulders in the manner of Spanish males. Along the streets the doors of the cottages were thrown open, the blinds rolled up, and small television screens flickered in the front rooms of those families who could afford them. Otherwise people sat outside and visited with their neighbors while the children ran around laughing and shouting until midnight or later. In the old days life happened in the streets.

During those years I was bewitched by the magic of the night: The softness of the evening air caressing my skin, the fragrance of night blooming jasmine as it floated like a cloud through which I walked. Silent, shuttered houses behind wrought iron, gated gardens, lined the streets where I passed. They were mysterious: Who were the families who inhabited their rooms and where had they gone? But it was the fragrance of those white blossoms spilling over the garden walls, profligate and generous, that filmed my nostrils, my skin, hair and my heart with its heady, voluptuous scent. The night sang with a million voices of crickets and other nocturnal creatures waking after the oppressive heat of the day. Night rules in southern Spain and all that has been listless and stupefied by the indolence of rising temperatures was now revitalized and revived, even the human heart and soul. The river that flowed languidly west of town was a hot spot of nightly activity: owls hooting, field mice scurrying to safety, the crickets singing, and beetles and mosquitoes darting about. What a glorious time it was to be young with all the veins and arteries pumping lustily and on high alert for the look, the touch, the hidden messages of courtship.

Night still rules all over Andalucía. The Spanish strollers still congregate at twilight for their evening paseo along Fuengirola's broad boulevard, the Paseo Marítimo, Príncipe de España. I have a color photograph of a group of beautiful Spanish horses, their manes and tails braided with red and yellow satin ribbons—the colors of the Spanish flag—as they paraded to dedicate this thoroughfare to the soon-to-be King of Spain, Juan Carlos. My white stallion, Favorito, was the most beautiful of the lot. I wasn't asked to ride him but whether it was because I was a woman or an *extranjera*, a non-Spaniard, I never knew.

In the summer, Spanish families still flock to Fuengirola from Spain's sweltering inland cities, just as they have done for generations. Their children are dressed for promenading: slicked back hair and crisp shorts for the boys, plaid sundresses and shiny Mary Janes for the girls. The babies in their strollers still suck on pacifiers, but the modern ones are big plastic thumbprints obscuring tiny baby faces. The tradition of the old grandmothers dressed in black, *en luto*—the stigmata of their widowhood—has all but disappeared. Now I see the grandmothers like Carmela wearing stylish high-heeled sandals, silk blouses in bright colors and luxurious Swiss watches on their wrists, their hair styled auburn, brunette or shiny black.

I had almost forgotten how years ago our fair hair and blue eyes would make the town's residents stop and stare. Now foreigners are ubiquitous and come by the rowdy planeload for a cheap blue-collar adventure on the Costa del Sol. Their languages—German, Dutch and Cockney—loop about each other in the warm night air. Now if Spaniards stare it's at the tourists' pale flesh turned scarlet by an overdose of sun, spilling out of ample bosoms and too short shorts, glowing phosphorescent in the fading light.

I see them all but hear instead across the decades the handclaps of groups of gypsy men *tocando palmas*, the sharp staccato of their palm beats ricocheting off the walls of our street as they danced along in the dead of night, singing their minor key melodies. I used to slip out of bed, pull back the floor-length shutters and press my face between the *rejas*— the iron grates over the windows—to look down on their joyous celebration of life. I can still hear their laughter and the clicks of their high-heeled boots on asphalt. Their haunting melodies would float awhile on the still night air as they turned the corner and were gone.

Here in Fuengirola's plaza, where Lauren and Lisa used to roller-skate round and round spitting *pipa* shells as they went, I see a flicker of recognition in the eyes of a gray-haired man who sells the tastiest sunflower seeds and toasted corn nuts—*pipas and kikos*—in the family *kiosco*. Yes, he remembers me when I jiggle his memory. He is the oldest brother of a young girl, Maribel, to whom I taught English in the classes I used to hold in our patio. I taught the children vocabulary by playing games like "Simon Says" and by helping them to write letters inviting the Queen of England to tea. Oh the fun we used to have together, my students and I, taking turns being "Simon" while darting and freezing in place around the old well. Life is easier now, he tells me. Maribel is a married woman with a big house and garden, and he has a BMW parked around the corner.

I walk the streets searching for ghosts and memories of my children's childhood, trying to make peace with the young, imperfect woman I was. But all the familiar places have changed and grown, as I too have changed and grown after so many years. Can I seriously begrudge the town and all its children and grandchildren this headlong rush to prosperity? Isn't it their turn to enjoy the abundance and materialism of modernity? And don't we all in the end have to learn to forgive ourselves and make peace with the selves we have been? Intellectually I understand the progress and development that democracy and tourism have brought. But it's from some other place deep inside me that I need to write this love letter to the town that helped shape me. Still, returning home to places you once loved is not for the faint of heart. They have left so few of the village's old roots to show through that a visitor can't even be certain they are in Spain. As I look down at the coast from the village of Mijas in the hills above, the beginnings and endings of Fuengirola are no longer visible. It's one huge urban spill, shaken out like pick-up-sticks, all along the coast.

Pepe's pottery, where I spent so many blissful hours up to my elbows in clay, is gone now, too. The thick whitewashed walls of the wood-fired ovens have been bulldozed back to the dust from which they came. I don't know what happened to the blue-tiled image of the Virgin that had reigned over the door of the large oven—"Carmen" he called it in honor of Carmela—for nearly eight decades. The year 1897 had been deeply etched into the oven's wall. Pepe called them "*hornos*" ovens, what we call a kiln. I like to think that before the bulldozers rumbled in, he chiseled that blue tile out and wrapped it in the old cloth where he kept the faded deed to the pottery and the old leather coin pouch that had belonged to his father, José Cano, for whom he was named. That deed has bought Pepe and Carmela's children spacious country houses, beachfront flats and luxury autos. He'd be pleased to know the comfort his family now enjoys. When I think of the deep affection Carmela and I share, I know it would make Pepe grin.

Bonfires no longer burn at night in the gypsy camp. Those blazing fires, around which the families used to gather to sing and dance, cast weird shadows along the thick, cinderblock walls that separated their camp from Pepe's pottery. Many nights, after the children were in bed, I'd slip down to the pottery to feed my horse, Arés, and to watch the gypsies dance around their fires. I'm pretty sure they never noticed me lost in the shadows, peering over the top of the wall as they clapped their hands in the sharp-hollow staccato that is for me the heartbeat of Andalucía. The little children and the bulbous women were the best dancers: the girls in raggy dresses, their skinny arms and legs mere twigs, and the boys wearing oversized pants hitched up at the waist with rope. They'd all take turns jumping into the center of the circle, flames elongating their shadows into El Greco blue figures. And with their supple young bodies and nimble bare feet stamping the dust, they would embody all the magic and seduction of the dance, which had been a part of their lives since the day they were born.

Yet I liked best the old women with bulging bodies and thick, blue-veined legs, like oak trees at the knees. With their dark eyes darting and hips swaying, while lifting frayed skirt hems provocatively, they were transformed into sensual beings of beauty and grace. It was on those nights, there in the darkness, that I first glimpsed the fierce, lusty power of women. "Sha sha sha," they'd hiss as their hips twitched and their fingers beckoned. How I loved those "*gordas*" around their fires. As I headed home, the light from the flames would make the fat rats scurrying along the tops of the walls and silhouetted on the tin roof of the pottery look like malevolent giants, a Goya etching come to life. Now their dilapidated camp, home to countless families of multiple generations, has been dredged clean and paved over. Where, I wonder, did all those Gypsy families go?

Some things remain however, that time and prosperity haven't erased. On clear mornings, just after sunrise, when the sky has curdled into pools of liquid color, if I look carefully, I can see the looming hulk of the great Rock of Gibraltar directly west. And if I peer intently south, across the molten waters of the Mediterranean, I can just make out the faint eyebrow of Algeria's coastline. And at twilight, if I turn my back on all this change and face the sea and squint my eyes just so, I can see only the melting of water and sky into one seamless, cerulean blue. And I am an uncertain young woman once again, all the old friends return, and the years drop away.

MAKING *LIMONADA*

Making *Limonada*

If tomorrow be sad or never come at all,
at least we've had today.
— Inscribed on a gold-plated bracelet, M.J.H. to D.L.H., 8.2.60

A motorcycle heading home from work past midnight skidded on winter's frozen center line, sending its twenty-four-year-old rider slamming into a stand of stately old California bay laurel trees, crushing his spleen. It was the day before Thanksgiving, 1962. At the emergency room they gave him a transfusion prescribed by an aging family doctor who knew little of treating trauma. One of his arteries burst and he bled to death.

The phone continued its incessant ring in my dream until I answered it. The doctor on the line told me that my grandfather was dead. As I struggled awake, trying to shake off the crushing state of gloom, I realized that the porch light was still on and the phone still ringing. I slid from the bed and ran, bare feet on the old pine floors, to hear Dr. Russell's voice telling me that Mark, my young husband, had had an accident and that I had better come to the hospital. Quickly?

Did he tell me to come quickly and I didn't hear him? Perhaps he didn't or I couldn't grasp the seriousness of his call.

"Do you want me to call Mark's parents?" he asked.

"No," I mumbled, "I'll call them."

But I didn't call them, at least not right away. It was midnight; numbed by the dream and stunned by his call I couldn't think. It took me time to find someone to take my two sleeping children. First I tried my mother who lived in a trailer on our property. She didn't respond to my frantic knocks and calls at her door.

"Mother, if I've ever needed you, I need you now," I pleaded into the frosty night. She either didn't hear me or didn't want to answer.

Then I tried our neighbors, Dick and Don, who lived in a cottage behind our house. They were apologetic but unable to help. Finally I rang the bell of the woman across the street. She stood in her bathrobe under the yellow porch light blinking the sleep from her eyes; she agreed to take the children. I carried them over, David, almost three, then Lisa, nearly four, and handed them into her waiting arms. Then I called Mark's parents. And by the time I drove over White's Hill and down Sir Francis Drake Boulevard to Marin General Hospital, the community hospital a half hour drive north of San Francisco, imagining all the while the sheepish grin that Mark would beam at me from his hospital bed for having crashed his precious red bike…by the time I walked down the hall into the emergency room, I could see in his father's face the truth that would forever change our lives.

Mark had called me about eight o'clock during his dinner break. I had grumbled as he munched his hamburger in my ear. I'd like to think he ordered a cheeseburger, fries and a milkshake, but I'm sure his wallet was empty. We talked about how much we both looked forward to Thanksgiving. A family day with our two young children. It hadn't been an easy time for us. We were still kids with more responsibility than our young shoulders could comfortably carry. In the early hours of Wednesday morning he would die. We never know what will be our last supper.

When morning came I wandered away from his parent's home calling Mark's name, stumbling along sidewalks glazed gold and red with autumn leaves, in a daze, at war with reality. I was certain that if I just looked in the right places I would find him. The young man with the hands that could make any old thing work again, the one who had a gentle manner with dogs and a goose, the boyish youth who told me that in grammar school the kids had taunted him and called him "Marshmallow Hershey Bar" so he changed his name from Marshall to Mark, the boy who loved a Siamese cat who would bound over the roof-tops and slip in through his bedroom window. "*Puta*," he called her. Whore, the first word I learned in Spanish. Dead? It did not happen. It could not be.

Mark Hirsch had stepped off a Greyhound Bus and into my life when I was sixteen. His brown hair and Mediterranean profile simply stamped their image indelibly in the corneas of my eyes and in the memory center of my brain. The cilia in my nose may have caught a whiff of his pheromones as he passed. One brief passing in the bus station on the way to our respective high schools. That was all. Who can explain the power of attraction, capricious and unpredictable, particularly when we are young and ripe with life?

Mark Hirsch on his 18th birthday, Stinson Beach

We were married the year after I graduated high school, while Mark finished his military service. My mother had wanted me to go to college and have a better life than she had had. But I had other ideas, and thought I knew best. The babies came quickly: first Lisa, nine months and five days after our wedding, then David, eleven and a half months later. With only a high school education Mark's work options were limited. We moved frequently, following his jobs, but always to remote dusty places. One summer, when he worked for the forest service, I was alone with my baby daughter five days and nights a week. We lived in the Sierra foothills where the nearest town was a tiny post office and a one-room store that sold dusty cans of soup and a two pack of Chun King chow mein. The refrigerated case hummed ceaselessly but the rusted shelves were empty. I don't know how I managed the silence of so many hours and days alone.

Just before David was born we moved again to a rustic cottage amid the sparsely populated rolling hills of the San Geronimo Valley. I washed the babies' diapers in an old pewter tub with an eggbeater center that swished back and forth, then I cranked each diaper through rollers by hand. I hung them on a clothesline and that winter, when I pulled them in, the diapers were frozen stiff, like sheets of ironed wax paper.

Mark would come home from work and head out to his beloved workshop where he would tinker away his spare time. Those were the years before fathers took an active role in their babies' lives. I thought that keeping a tidy house was more important than getting silly with my babies. Often short tempered with fatigue I didn't know enough to ask for Mark's help. In our last year he showed me what he had written while sitting on a creek bank. Scribbled on a scrap of paper he had tried to express his struggles with the responsibilities he had assumed too quickly.

It was a shock to see my young husband cold and dead. Flowers sent in sympathy emitted a sickly sweet smell. His hands, folded neatly on his chest, felt like marble. As I ran my fingers over his body, nothing yielded softly as it had forty-eight hours before. The light in the mortuary was not natural light. The sounds were not normal sounds of life but hushed and cushioned. People whispered. There was no laughter.

Mark had served two years in the Marine Corps; he was entitled to a military funeral. In his 24th year, I committed my young husband to a windswept grave at the National Cemetery in South San Francisco where the white head-stones contrast starkly with the rolling green hills. I wore the navy blue, short-sleeved silk dress that I'd worn when we'd become engaged. I didn't own a coat. A young Marine in dress blues played taps, the bugle's mournful notes hung for a while in the gray cover of clouds. They folded the flag that had covered his coffin and handed it to me, a heavy cotton triangle of red, white and blue. I escaped into the blessed oblivion of sleep, leaning into his uncle's shoulder during the long drive back to his parents' house.

By the time I drove home over the mountain to San Geronimo it was night, the rain hard and steady. At the sight of Mark's boots waiting expectantly in the kitchen, I broke down.

"Stop your crying," hissed my mother. "All your life you've been a cry baby. Stop your crying for the sake of the children." I escaped sobbing into the darkness, away from her harsh judgments, and knocked again on the door of our neighbors, Dick and Don. They took me in, sat me down in front of their fire, and handed me a stiff drink and some kind of pill.

There was no embracing family to act as an anchor through the turbulence. Mark's parents had lost their only son and moved away within weeks. It was "too hard for his father to see the children," offered his mother in explanation. I didn't understand why my own mother just disappeared;

it would be a decade before I had enough distance to even hazard a guess. I'd never known my father and since I was an only child, there were no siblings to turn to. One of the questions that has plagued me over the years is how a whole rural community could have allowed a young family facing such a tragic loss to bear the pain alone. Perhaps the answer is that I just don't remember and that there really were wonderful acts of kindness and reaching out. But I have absolutely no recollection of any. More probably, the situation was too tragic and inexplicable and no one knew what to say or do, so they did nothing.

Here is what I do recall: The cards, the notes and the flowers at Mark's funeral. I remember that their fragrance mixed with the smell of embalming fluid lay heavy on the air. I have mercifully pushed that smell out of my memory but I would know it again in an instant. It is the smell of death. I recall the gray note cards edged in a deeper gray that Mark's grandmother gave me so that I could write thank you notes to all the people who sent large floral sprays in condolence. I never wrote those thank you notes. I had neither the energy nor the will.

In the second or third dark week, I drove up with the children to visit Mark's aunt and uncle, at their ranch outside Marysville. One early morning when the winter day was still just a faint promise, I saw a silvery fox dancing out on the lawn. Watching him, I felt certain that Mark's spirit had gone to inhabit some wild and beautiful creature like that fox. That thought gave me comfort for a brief moment. But I was restless and needed to be on the move. So the children and I drove home again to San Geronimo in our little aqua VW Bug. On the way down Highway 80 we stopped at the Milk Farm Restaurant. I remember blurting out to the waitress who brought our food that my husband had just been killed on a motorcycle. Poor woman. What an awful burden I thrust upon her, but I needed to talk to someone about my pain. I must have been trying on for size the reality and finality of Mark's death.

I ran a high fever on Christmas Day, drifting in and out of sleep, unable to move much beyond the couch. Still in their pajamas, Lisa and David curled up with me, the three of us huddled together on the sofa for comfort. Who fed my children? Who fed the dogs, Laddie and Brandy, the golden Basset Hound? Who fed Louie the goose and Sidney our duck? Perhaps no one.

There was a knock on the door sometime during that blurry period. A young man who had served with Mark in the Marine Corps was traveling through California and stopped by to say hello to his friend. As he stood on the doorstep I blurted out that Mark was dead. The suddenness with which I hit him with the news shocked even me. Did I invite him in to have a cup of tea and talk? I don't remember.

Then there was the matter of Mark's dog. His name was Laddie, an Australian Shepherd. We'd gotten him as a six-week-old puppy. He disappeared about six weeks after Mark died. I searched the neighborhood and put up signs. Later I figured out that he must have followed my mother when she walked away and out of our lives, not to reappear again for at least a dozen years. She had been kind to him as she was to all four-legged creatures. She had fed him when I forgot. By the time I went to the Humane Society, they said they had destroyed him the day before. That kind of distress cannot be good for a growing fetus.

Many of the memories I have of our short life together are punishing. One afternoon, not long before he died,

Mark's mother and his grandmother had driven out for a visit. Suddenly it was time for Mark to leave for work and he needed to eat before he began his evening shift, which started at 3:30 and ended at 11:30 p.m. In those days I wasn't much of a cook, although I did make a mean cheese soufflé that puffed up reliably. But this day I wasn't making soufflés and I had to make something. So, with my cheeks burning with embarrassment for being caught so unprepared... this meal was after all for their son and grandson and I was taking care of him poorly. I found a frozen meat patty in the big freezer that was nearly empty, threw it into a frying pan that sputtered and spattered on the stove. I stood watching it with my back to the three of them so they wouldn't see my shame. Then I put it on a plate and served it with a bottle of A-1 sauce and a glass of milk. I remember his mother and grandmother looking on and mercifully not commenting on my poor offering. And my husband didn't make a word of protest or complaint. I don't know if this was because of the presence of his family so as not to embarrass me or if he truly did not mind that that was all there was to eat. No nice green salad, no fresh vegetables, no bowl of homemade soup or chili. He deserved better.

"You never seemed to want to talk about the death of our father," my oldest daughter said to me years later, when she was a grown woman, older than I had been at the time. She was right. How was I to explain to my children that I never wanted anyone's pity? I didn't want our lives to fly so out of control. How does one explain to one's children the splintering effect of such a death? How to explain the experience of being abruptly alone at twenty-three, with two children under five and pregnant? And survival and running away from the places and the memories took up the next years.

And, after a while, one doesn't ever want to go back, even in the mind. Under the circumstances the choices were stark: wilt or make the proverbial lemonade. I made *limonada*, as they call it in Spain.

Marshall John Hirsch II, a tiny Marshmallow Hershey Bar, was born on my birthday, August 2nd, 1963. What a birthday gift he was. I looked into his newborn eyes and saw the wisdom of an old soul. That baby gave me back my will to live. When Marshall was just three months old, November 24, 1963, a year and two days after Mark died, another young widow stood numbly erect, her small daughter and son just Lisa and David's ages, watching their father's funeral caisson roll by. The entire world mourned his loss, yet I, who should have been able to empathize, looked on as if from a great distance.

Lisa, Diana, David and baby Marshall

By early the following year I had to flee. Deeply ashamed by the failure of Mark's death, I was too haunted by its images. Meanwhile, Narin—I hardly knew her but she was my age and the daughter of Narin and Stuart Rasmussen who had been like surrogate parents to me—had written me saying, "Don't stay in California and join the PTA. Come to Spain." I began to feel that I had a responsibility to live life for both of us, that my eyes had to drink in the world for Mark, too. I saw absolutely no obstacles to a 24-year-old woman with three small children flying to New York and boarding an Italian liner, steerage class, to Spain. I had a little insurance money and a big need to escape. The benefit of not having a nurturing family was that there was no one to disagree.

Soon we were lurching along the passageways of the Italian liner *Leonardo da Vinci*, crossing the Atlantic bound for Gibraltar. I was pushing the stroller with the ten-month-old baby, Marshall, while my small son, David, and his sister, Lisa, hugged my hem. I was giggling about our predicament. We were lost, always lost in these endless corridors. It was probably the first time in a long time that my children had heard me laugh. We were four young swimmers adrift, heading up to the sunlight and fresh air, up to a deck full of Fulbright scholars heading to Europe. I was just their age. One in particular, Gloria Feiman from New York City, had a splash of honeyed freckles across her cheeks and was going to Madrid where she was to live with a Spanish señora for a year. Gloria and I became pals during that crossing and exchanged letters for years.

Fortunately Italian liners served wine with lunch and dinner. It helped round the edges and gave me a pleasant buzz. Our cabin, down in the bowels of the ship, was so small that I had to dress the children in shifts. The sister and her brother waited out in the corridor while I dressed the baby and myself. With the baby's porta-crib there wasn't room to stand. I never knew if it was night or day since there were no portholes in steerage class. I think we slept through many meals.

On the Leonardo da Vinci

I asked the purser to direct us to the children's playroom with nannies and toys as promised in the glossy brochure. He directed me to a colorful room but it was empty. No toys, no books, and no nanny. The brochure neglected to mention that supervised play was a perk only for cabin and first class passengers. That discovery was a disappointment that brought me to tears. I pleaded for a few hours of child-care and gave him a peek at how ragged I felt. I'm sure I told him that all of our waking hours I was sole caretaker of three young children and I felt worn out by the strain. So he allowed the two older children to join in the play activities upstairs in cabin class for a few hours a day. Then the baby would crawl around my feet as I sat in a deck chair, taking in the air and feeling grateful for the tiny slice of freedom from responsibility.

We disembarked in Gibraltar. A big tender came out to meet the ship and took us and our mammoth black trunk to meet Narin. She had said we could stay with her for a while. I was unable to see the obvious: I was running away from pain, from the telephone, from memories, from mortuaries, abandonment and death. In Spain I wouldn't have to drive past places where there were dead bodies laid out in the middle of flowers and wreaths. Heading off to Spain when I didn't speak more than a handful of Spanish words would challenge my ingenuity. But then, out of necessity, I'd had loads of that since childhood.

Some friends of Narin's came with a car and drove us east toward Málaga and the town of Fuengirola. The sea shimmered like a sequined robe. What would someday be known world-wide as the glittering Costa del Sol, was still a series of small fishing villages connected by kilometers of empty ivory beaches with hardly an apartment complex in sight.

For a few weeks we shared Narin's second-floor apartment in town. What I loved about that apartment was its smell: clean, fragrant, soft and comforting. The fragrance of Dove soap. (Ironically, her apartment was across the narrow street from number 28 José Antonio, the wonderful old house we would later call home for many years.) In a next memory we are sitting in the sunny seats at a bullfight in Marbella. We had taken the local bus, the older two children and I. We must have made quite a spectacle as we climbed to our cheap seats in the bullring. We were Scandinavian fair and blue-eyed. We did not blend in. Men seated around us smiled and attempted to make conversation with the flaxen-haired mother and her young blond children. Attempting to return the courtesy of conversation I announced "*estoy caliente*" in my best Spanish but only succeeded in announcing that I was in heat.

I rented a large villa—La Cancela—at the east end of town, a few steps from the beach. My room was on the second floor with shutters that opened to the sunlight and the sea. The sound of the waves and the fresh winds off the Mediterranean were a balm. Rosa Diaz, a widow with a young daughter and an elderly, frail gardener came with the house. Rosa was an excellent cook and made delicious paella with which we all fell in love, especially cold for breakfast. On those mornings I'd hand the kids spoons and pull the leftovers from the fridge. We'd hover over the dish, scooping out golden-hued grains of rice flecked with strands of saffron, small chunks of chicken and tiny clams, still nestled in half open shells. Rosa cooked, cleaned, and scrubbed our clothes in a large cement sink outside the kitchen. She was a steady, loving presence in our lives. Salvador, the greengrocer, came by each morning in his putt-putt van that sputtered to a stop outside our arched, wrought iron gate. Rosa and the children and I would race out to see what vegetables, fruit and fish he was bringing around that day.

David, Marshall and Rosa choosing bread

"*Panaderoooooooo,*" sang out the bread man, the long oohs somersaulting along the stuccoed walls and tiled rooftops. His three-wheeled van looked like the one that held the dead bodies in the French film *Diabolique.* He brought sweet, fresh bread and the children loved to run out to choose a loaf. David, in his little bedroom off the kitchen, started hoarding bread under his pillow. I like to think he took it out in the middle of the night and its fragrance comforted a four-year-old in the dark. Our old gardener cared for the lawn and the rampant bougainvillea and jasmine. He would bend his long skinny frame over to take the baby's hands and teach him to walk across the lawn. Marshall had his first birthday in this house.

Lisa and Diana

I didn't wear black and although we were alone without a husband and father, we didn't stand out in the painful way I had experienced at home. Nobody felt sorry for me. The Spaniards were pragmatic. After all, just twenty-five years before, they had survived their brutal Civil War. Fuengirola was full of men and women wearing black. The whole country was still numb, mourning their dead and the tens of thousands of disappeared. Birth and death happened. I was just another young widow, alone with her children in the land of the bereaved.

Lisa, Marshal and David in Moroccan chilabas

The sound of the clop-clop-clopping of burros' and mules' hooves outside our windows filtered in like welcome dust, settling comfortably around my shoulders. In that big black trunk I had brought along a small record player and some old LPs. I played Rachmaninov's Piano Concerto No. 3 in D minor over and over again. The beauty of the music seeped in and soothed me. I had stopped crying.

Before dawn one morning I slipped out through the garden and quietly closed the massive, wrought iron gate. I left the children behind with Narin and Rosa and caught a ride to Madrid with Sacha, a Russian artist whom I scarcely knew. "Sacha, Artist by the grace of gods" his card read. He was having an exhibition in Madrid. I attended the opening of his show in a gallery full of elegantly dressed Spaniards, men and women with the most marvelous haughty posture. I saw Gloria and another of my Fulbright friends from the ship and listened to them talk of classes at the university and funny stories of fitting in to a Spanish family. It seemed to me as though their days of scholarship were like a dream, living as they did in high-ceilinged apartments with balconies that overlooked the throbbing, tree-lined city. And returning late at night, I would stand with them in front of their building while they clapped their hands sharply to the empty streets. An echoing response of a stout staff striking the ground and from out of dark recesses the *sereno* would come running with his huge set of keys, throwing open the massive front door that led to a rococo, gilt elevator. I saw this kaleidoscope life in Madrid as enchanted, and felt giddily as though I had been touched by a magic wand just by getting a glimpse. Insatiable, I jumped at the chance to ride the Talgo, an overnight train to Lisbon with one of the young Americans for a weekend of sightseeing. After a week of trying on the life of being young—a week in which I heard lithe Spanish men singing love songs to blond American girls and saw how life billowed into the streets until daybreak—I headed back to my small family. In my absence David had tried to burn the cat with a hot stick from the fireplace. I scared him thoroughly by grabbing him and threatening to show him firsthand what it would feel like to be burned. In the glowing red firelight I could see fear in his eyes but could not feel his pain and bewilderment. I could only feel my own.

The sunlight was endless, the first thing to greet me in the morning. It illuminated our garden until my eyes drooped at night. It was as though all the light was helping restore some internal equilibrium. Our old life seemed blessedly far away. I could pretend to forget my story, my children's story. There would be another husband and another child someday. But for the moment there was no future. I had no memories and no dreams.

Now We Are Six

*Twenty years from now you will be more
disappointed by the things you didn't do than by
the things you did do. So throw off the bowlines,
push away from the safe harbor, catch the trade
winds in your souls. Explore. Dream. Discover.*

— Mark Twain

Before the children and I left for Spain, I was invited
to my friend Ann Karren's family Passover Seder. At
their large oval table with its heavy white damask
cloth I was seated between two men. On my right, Malcolm
Cohen, a rosy-cheeked Englishman who hadn't been in the
U.S. terribly long, and on my left, Bob Cohn, Ann's cousin.
By the end of the evening Bob had asked me on a date. I
said yes but immediately had second thoughts since I hadn't
dated and the prospect made me anxious. After a few days of
discomfort I called Bob and cancelled, and heaved a sigh of
relief. I clearly wasn't ready.

A few weeks later Ann invited me to go skiing with a small
group of her friends. I'd been a good skier in high school and
this sounded like fun. So I asked Katie, a grandmother who
used to work for Mark's parents, to come for the weekend to

look after the children. Malcolm from the Seder was along on the weekend with his girlfriend. Unfortunately, she broke her leg skiing the first day. However, he treated her so nicely and was such a warm person and so easy to talk to, that when he called me some weeks later and invited me to an ice hockey game I said yes. This time I didn't have misgivings since I already thought of him as a friend. When he came to my house the first time he sat down on the couch and our basset hound, Brandy, promptly threw up right beside his shoes. Malcolm didn't seem overly excited by what had happened. I was favorably impressed. He was also quite jolly with my children and loved to throw the ball and run around with them in the park on weekends. I introduced Malcolm to Mark's parents when we drove up for a visit one weekend with the children.

Nonetheless, I planned to go to Spain, and had no trouble sticking with the plan, no matter how charming the Englishman. Narin's words "Don't stay and join the PTA" kept going through my head. Such a future seemed intolerably bleak and just the thought of it caused me to feel trapped.

After the children and I arrived in Fuengirola, Malcolm and I exchanged a few letters and talked several times via a central *kiosco telefónico*, a bank of black receivers and mouthpieces on the beachfront in Fuengirola, staffed by a young Spanish woman who would plug a cord into her switchboard when it was my turn to take a call. Then I'd hurry to the wall and shout into the mouthpiece hoping to be heard over the din of everyone else's animated conversations. Somewhat to my surprise, Malcolm called me in November of that year and suggested we get married. Without thinking it through thoroughly, I said yes. After all, he was a lovely man and he would make a good father for my children. So I hauled the four of us and the big black steamer trunk to London to meet his mother and father and then back to San Francisco. Despite serious doubts about what I was about to do—doubts that had nothing to do with Malcolm and everything to do with me not wanting to commit myself again—I buried my anxiety and we were married on December 27, 1964, two years after Mark's death.

Malcolm brought a joyful and buoyant spirit into our emotionally starved lives. He was the sort of man who opened a bunch of tin cans, threw their contents together into a big pot, stirred and heated up the mess and served it in big bowls and gave it some alluring and mouth-watering name. Then he plopped it on the table along with piles of white bread and heaps of butter. Abundance. That's what Malcolm brought into our lives. Emotional abundance. He danced, he sang, he held one-sided conversations with an empty orange juice tin, holding the can to his ear to hear its whispered responses. What an energetic and big-hearted spirit he brought to the famished emotional likes of my little family.

Until he was in his mid-twenties and emigrated to the U.S., Malcolm had been a Boy Scout leader in London. Taking on me and my young family of two boys and a girl was just like being a scout leader. He had such a wealth of motherly qualities that it allowed me to shift some of the weighty responsibilities off my shoulders on to his. And lord knows, at times I desperately needed the warmth and loving care of a good mother. The trouble would come later when I was ready to be treated like a grown-up. But I couldn't see that then.

After a few months of living in a large flat in San Francisco I bought a house in Marin with the proceeds from the sale of my San Geronimo house. Despite having a new husband and a new home, I was emotionally unsettled. I developed what I can only call a severe case of amnesia. I desperately needed to pretend that Mark had never died and that tragedy had never been a part of our lives. When friends would ask how Malcolm and I met I would make up stories, anything to keep from telling the truth of my life. I didn't want anyone knowing that Malcolm wasn't the children's father so I enrolled them in school using his surname, Cohen, instead of their father's surname, Hirsch. We would quarrel about my lies and my unwillingness to tell people what had happened. Malcolm couldn't understand.

"Why can't you just tell them the truth?" he'd ask. "Why do you have to make up stories? What are you trying to hide?"

"I can't explain it to you if you don't understand," I'd say tearfully, groping for a logic that eluded me. "It's my life and my history and I don't owe anyone an explanation."

The truth, as I now understand it, was that I didn't want anyone feeling sorry for me. I didn't want to feel that because I'd been widowed that I was different. I'd wrestled with being different all my life, being raised as I was in the patrician town of Ross by a single mother who worked as a cleaning lady in the fancy estates. I just wanted what everyone else seemed to have—a regular family.

Even though I had lost my husband and, in effect, my mother as a result of one tragic accident, for Malcolm the pieces just didn't add up. It's not that he wasn't caring and supportive but hiding secrets was something he couldn't fathom. He thought he knew best how I should handle the truth of my life. On the surface at least, I had what I thought I needed: a normal family without a past. Yet inside I was still haunted by Mark's death, only I had it all so securely stuffed down that I couldn't even feel the feelings. I scrunched my eyes tightly each time I drove past a mortuary. Once in a while a sad movie or TV show that dealt with death would break open the dam inside me and the pain would come from someplace so deep that it threatened to swallow me whole. At times like that I desperately wanted to physically flee the places that held such unhappy memories. What I didn't recognize was that numbness and depression were the price I paid for avoiding my grief. Still, I was doing the best I could with the skills and understanding I had.

Malcolm and Diana, Mill Valley

The financial decisions I'd made after Mark's death and the stocks and mutual funds I'd inherited from his estate, Malcolm took to calling my "old wrinkled family retainers," chiding me for being unwilling to actively trade them. I resented his insistence that he had better business judgment than I, since he had zero investments of his own. Yet I was worn down by his arguments wrapped in the cloak of humor. Eventually I relented and consented to Malcolm placing my investments with a stockbroker friend of his who had been his roommate, putting the account in our joint names. He once told me that when he came to America he pictured himself marrying a blond woman with money, children, and driving a station wagon. At the time we each got what we thought we needed.

In the meantime, Malcolm's father died in London of a heart attack. He and his dad hadn't been particularly close but he was a loyal son and his father's death was a big loss. It was also a terrible time in America with the assassination first of Martin Luther King and then, less than two months later, Robert Kennedy. The nightly television showed pictures of flag-draped caskets returning from Vietnam and the whole country seemed a madhouse: riots in the streets, protests against the war, civil rights marches, police brutality…it was a terrible time. Back in 1963 I had marched in San Francisco with Lisa and David, pushing Marshall in the baby buggy when he was six weeks old, to protest the bombing of the Birmingham, Alabama church that killed four young Sunday school girls. So it wasn't the public outrage and demonstrations that were disturbing. It was all the senseless death. It seemed as though our country had gone quite mad; I found it destabilizing and unsettling. All was not well with my country just as all was not well with me.

I figured I could afford to lure us all away if we sold the house and relied on my Social Security survivors' benefits. From my time in Spain I knew that village life agreed with me. In flight from my past and the trauma of American life, hitting the road seemed a perfect tonic for whatever it was that ailed me. At the time Malcolm was a salesman for an American lumber company and although he had the perfect jolly, joke-telling personality for the job, he hated the rejection involved in sales, and was more than happy to chuck it all in and join me on the "big adventure." We would be taking, as we explained to our friends, "a moratorium on decisions." No more house payments, bills or insurance, at least for a long while.

Once again the children and I set sail, this time on the British liner, *Arcadia*, under the soaring towers of the Golden Gate Bridge. This time there were six of us instead of my original four, since we now had a chubby toddler, Lauren, who had her father's English rosy cheeks and Dumbo ears. It was late June 1969.

Heading off on an ocean voyage promised to be a happy time being vagabonds from regular life. We disembarked ship in Southampton on July 20, 1969. A new red VW camper with a pop-top was waiting for us on the dock. That night we all stood outside under the full moon gazing up at its glory as Neil Armstrong's voice crackled back to earth,

"Tranquility Base here...That's one small step for man, one giant leap for mankind."

In our van we peregrinated leisurely about the countryside of England, Scotland and Wales, sleeping in hay fields and farmers' pastures and cooking our meals on a green Coleman camping stove, its blue flame hissing promisingly. On our first night, dinner was a rotund pale green cabbage pilfered from a field, chopped up and added to a package of Knorr's Potato & Leek soup. The picture in my memory is of the six of us sitting on the ground by the side of the lane with our legs stuck out in front of us, our noses buried in brightly colored enamel mugs, breathing in the moist fragrance of that hot cabbage soup in the open air. That night we ate like kings on the open road.

Sailing San Francisco to Southampton, P&O Arcadia

Marshall and Lauren

Our camper was a marvel of design, and with the table extended it became Chez Cohen, dispensing savory, one-pot meals. For a while we had an eighteen-year-old au pair traveling with us, and then we were seven. She slept in the pop-top, Malcolm and I on the double bed with Lauren at our heads, Lisa had an air mattress on the floor under our bed, there was a canvas hammock for David that extended above the two front seats and we propped up my typewriter and jackets and made a bed across the front seats underneath for Marshall.

With this kind of crowd shoehorned in, we had to abolish evening cups of tea and drinks of water after 5 p.m. Before prohibition, the middle of the night bathroom brigade traffic had been brisk. A sound night's sleep became difficult particularly if it was pouring outside and someone started wailing in the dark of night,

"I can't find my boots."

Before we drifted off to sleep at night Malcolm and I would take turns reading aloud. My favorite story was *The Wind in the Willows* and the hilarious adventures of Mr. Toad and his motorcar. Sometimes we were all laughing so hard that someone invariably developed the hiccups.

It was often raining as we meandered around Great Britain; we saw *Chitty Chitty Bang Bang* more times than I care to remember. We also ate an awful lot of fish and chips, one of us braving the chilly deluge to duck into a local shop, returning with newspaper cones of crisp chunks of plaice and chips (fries) drenched with vinegar and salt.

Several mornings in Scotland we hiked up to a castle on a craggy hilltop carrying our breakfast in a rucksack. Afternoons we'd often knock on a farmer's door and ask to spend the night camping in his field. We stayed six weeks in the field of a farmer and his wife in Wales and ended up becoming like members of their family. They fell in love with our children, especially David, so some mornings the farmer would head off on his big tractor with my flaxen-haired son beside him. We picked blackberries from the vines along the railway tracks and I made jam in a pot on our camp stove. There's a funny photo of little Lauren, sitting on her potty, out in the middle of that field. With the stability of being in one place for a while, we all took riding lessons on Welsh ponies; the whole family wore velvet black riding helmets as we learned to keep our heels down and sit deep in the English saddles.

Cool clean sheets and hot water became two things I swore I would never again take for granted. The longest we ever went without a bath was our time in Wales. We took daily sponge baths and changed our clothes frequently, and aside from the telltale rings around our necks, we stayed presentable. Finally we discovered the public bathhouse, a part of the local swimming pool in Aberystwyth. These rather ancient but scrupulously clean facilities dated from a time before indoor plumbing in homes, and public bathhouses were a necessity, particularly in the heavy mining and industrial areas of Wales. In the bathhouse we got a big tub full of steaming hot water, where we could stretch out our legs and soak, plus soap and a towel, all for what was then about 18 cents an hour. As we drove farther up into the Scottish Highlands around Fort William and Inverness, laundromats and public bathhouses became non-existent and we had to wash in the abundant streams that gargled and trilled down the wooded hillsides.

We were in Edinburgh during the fall Edinburgh Festival. Men in kilts strode the streets, flags flew everywhere and the city fairly crackled with plays and music, theatre, and an international stamp exhibition. For lunch we became addicted to hot meat pies from a little bakery on Bakers Place. Those meat pies were so deliciously oozing with flavor that I once did a little Highland fling of pleasure, much to the delight of the salesladies. We camped outside of town along the Firth of Forth within sight of Edinburgh's miniature version of the Golden Gate Bridge. One afternoon I bought a single remaining ticket to the symphony, left the children and Malcolm at the campground, and took myself out for a rare treat of classical music. Each evening "The Fish Supper Special" van parked outside the site and groups of campers came strolling back clutching their hot fish and chips wrapped in newsprint, licking the salt and vinegar from their fingers as they walked. It was a time when seven people could eat fish and chips without spending more than $2.50.

From the start I was quite intimidated by the old dowager cleaning ladies who watched over the public loos in Great Britain with an eagle eye. In one Edinburgh loo I began reading an article in a newspaper on the floor, and figuring I'd had more than my share of time, the matron put her key in the lock, the door flew open, and I found myself outside too astonished to even protest.

That fall we rented a house for a month in a town on the seacoast of Wales. One morning I spotted an ad in the *London Times*. "Seeking winter caretakers for an old *mas*— farmhouse—in Van Gogh's balmy Provence," it lured. I sent off a quick response saying that "I would gladly cut off an ear" for the chance to winter in Provence. It turned out the house was the summer residence of the poet Stephen Spender and his concert pianist wife, Natasha, and their insurance required the house be occupied for the policy to remain in effect. We were invited to meet the Spenders at their home on Abbey Road in London. I remember Stephen Spender carrying in a sponge cake that he had made to serve with tea. I had no idea he was such a famous poet. After securing the assignment, we made a rather rapid drive down to Provence, stopping in Paris for dinner on the Left Bank. What a thrill it was for me to finally set my eyes on all those famous sights, sharing it with the children and Malcolm. We drove right under the Eiffel Tower and the kids stood in their pajamas looking up its center, like a giant piece of sculptured lace. It was a Friday night and the streets were alive: the shops were open and the stalls filled with beautiful pastries, heaps of glistening fruit and vegetables, stylishly dressed people, small cars and big fat drops of rain that made the wet asphalt a refractory of a thousand colors. As a young girl I had stared at blue bottles of Evening in Paris cologne in the

Five and Dime; spending an evening in Paris was something I had never dared to dream.

The Spender's farmhouse—Mas St. Jérome—was a rambling structure with foot-thick stone walls set in olive groves at the top of a hill above the town of Maussane, halfway between Arles and Avignon. The mountains of Van Gogh's Les Alpilles rose like a jagged chalk-white graph line in the distance. Rosemary, thyme and lavender grew wild on the hills and I would often gather big fragrant armloads and fill jars around the house with their lovely color and pungent aroma. Most of the water came from a well, while the rest was gravity fed from a rain tank on the roof.

Shortly after we arrived, Natasha Spender flew down for a few days to make certain we were acquainted with the house and the environs and that we understood the tasks we were expected to complete. She asked Malcolm to plant an orchard of espaliered pear trees that would form the first bones of the extensive gardens she dreamed of. He had to water those young trees by hand, lugging buckets of water from the well. That first evening of her visit I was upstairs telling the children stories and they were laughing and giggling so much that I pinched them, hard enough to hurt, to get them to keep quiet. I was so intent on making a good impression on Madame Spender that I was willing to inflict pain on my own children.

The house had no electricity but we did have a noisy Honda generator that powered the lights for about four hours on one fill of gas. When the fuel ran out and blackness and silence suddenly dropped their thick mantle, one of us, usually Malcolm, had to race outside to fetch the generator and bring it under cover as per Natasha Spender's instructions. When Malcolm went to London for ten days I remember how scary it was to dash into the night with the Mistral howling through the cypress trees, their long black shadows dancing ominously in the ghostly clear air. That was the thing about the Mistral: It blew so fiercely it swept away everything on land and in the sky. Some nights we relied on paraffin lamps and candles for light and heat from the enormous stone fireplace that dominated the living room. The stones were pitted with fossilized sea creatures from some pre-historic time when the sea covered this region of France. When the Mistral blew its frigid breath down from the Alps, the old house slyly allowed the wind to slip through the gaps in her stones. The interior temperature would plummet so drastically that I often huddled together with the children, literally inside the fireplace, trying to stay warm. Since wood was expensive, every time we took a walk in the hills, Malcolm, the children and I would hunt for whatever we could find to burn and return like scavengers with our arms laden.

On a clear day from the top of Spender's Peak, as we named it, we could see south across the Rhone Valley to the marsh lands of the Camargue, to the snowy summit of Mont Ventoux and in the other direction to the ghostly ruins of the Abbaye de Montmajour on the road to Arles. On sunny days the sunlight would pour in through the large arched French doors and I could almost forget how icy it would turn by nightfall.

We enrolled Lisa, David and Marshall in the village school at no cost and with a minimum of formality considering how much the French seemed to love filling out forms. Because the children didn't speak French, their ability to join in lessons was limited to math and *écriture*—writing—and they brought home long lists of French vocabulary to study at night. For about fifty cents each they had a four course hot

MAKING *LIMONADA*

lunch served in the school cafétéria; they had only to bring along their own loaf of bread and a napkin. One week David and Lisa's class made crepes; I hoped the kids would have a class on the collecting and preparation of snails.

With the older children in school we took the opportunity to explore the Provençal countryside around Avignon, visiting Saint Rémy where Van Gogh had been a patient in the cloister of Saint Paul. It was still an asylum after all these years. The almond trees had just bloomed and the place looked just as it did in his paintings. A nun in a large, starched, white winged hat came outside to dry the salad greens for lunch. I watched her twirl her wire basket and thought that was probably just the way the greens were dried when Van Gogh had lived here. On another outing we picnicked at the Pope's Palace overlooking the famous Pont d'Avignon. Then we explored a couple of local wineries.

"Di, we have to go or we'll be late to pick up the kids," Malcolm reminded me.

"Oh come on, we have time for one more look," I'd responded carelessly. It's a day that haunts me still. We returned to Maussane at least an hour late. Lisa, David and Marshall had been left waiting in the frigid afternoon air. They didn't have winter coats or pocket money to go into the bakery or wait in the local café, so they stood, frozen and forlorn, waiting on the corner of the park for their parents to show up and collect them.

Wednesday and Saturday were market days in Arles and the fresh fruits and vegetables were scrubbed and arrayed like a county fair. The heaping stalls stretched on for blocks and somewhere on one edge was Van Gogh's tiny house where he painted Starry Night in Arles. It was great fun to stagger through the crowds, our wicker baskets bulging with all the fresh food we'd take home to cook. We'd stop to sample from the big crocks of olives and taste slivers of more variety of cheeses than I could have ever imagined. The proprietors of each stall seemed to try outdoing each other in the tastes and samples they offered. We'd buy a slice of homemade pizza and peer at all the live rabbits and chickens, turkeys and ducks, price the flowers and ferns and enjoy them all for free. Using a list of shellfish from an Elizabeth David cookbook that Natasha Spender had given me, I bought enough sea creatures to make bouillabaisse—a whole basket full, topped off with a sinister looking eel, who glared out from the top of my basket.

One busy Saturday, when the market was at its height of activity, we turned around and Lauren was gone, absolutely vanished. People stopped and peered around empathically in response to our calls but no Lauren. Suddenly someone pointed far ahead: There in the distance we could see the back of a rotund *gendarme* clutching tightly to the hand of a short little girl as he whisked her along as fast as her chubby little legs would go.

"Our baby…*notre petite fille,*" we called, dropping our baskets and running in hot pursuit. Of course. He was taking her to the local *gendarmerie,* thinking she was lost. Yet with the aplomb of a seasoned traveler, she seemed completely unruffled by her adventure and managed to give him a lovely smile as we breathlessly retrieved her and thanked him for his trouble.

We ate our Christmas dinner outside in the blazing warmth of the afternoon Provençal sun. It was about then that I experienced my first bout of what I took to be home-sickness, although I didn't know what it was I was homesick for. While I thoroughly relished all that was new and rustic in Provençal life, I still experienced a momentary twinge of longing for the familiar ways of my own culture. And then the feelings passed and never returned.

It was in a pool of sunlight that had collected on the living room floor that I read in the International Herald Tribune of the massacre of villagers in My Lai. I stayed in that sunny spot trying to get warm and wrote a poem to express my anguish, brushing away hot tears for those lost Vietnamese lives and for the young American soldiers who were also victims of a stupid and senseless war. It seemed clear to me, even then, that if you put soldiers into the terrible stress of war, some such tragedies were almost inevitable.

It was writing that poem that got me thinking about doing something with all the notes and scribbling I'd been keeping in my notebook. So I took a pale blue aerogram, filling every surface, every margin, with my observations about traveling in Europe with a family, using little money and heaps of ingenuity. I sent it off to the editor of Marin County's *Pacific Sun* newspaper. I was beyond delirious when he promptly wrote back and offered me a twice-monthly column in his paper.

Since our responsibilities included looking after the house, Malcolm hired Monsieur Pontex, Maussane's chimney sweep, to come and attend to the fireplace. The sweep—right out of a Dickens's novel—arrived on his old sputtering Mobylette motorbike. He had a battered bazooka shell, in which he kept his brushes, wired to the gas tank. If we had lit a match as he exhaled, Monsieur Pontex would have burst into flame from the alcohol on his breath.

The village was full of these colorful characters. Madam De Foe, the village washer lady, rolled her washing machine out in her front yard amid the chickens and ducks and cheerfully sudsed away. Another member of the large De Foe family was Bijou, a handsome 32-year-old Camargue horse who, until the year before, had pulled the town's garbage wagon and hearse. He wasn't retired because of his age but because the hearse and garbage collection were finally motorized. If you couldn't find your garbage can after collection from the main street, you went to see Papa Gypsy who took the unclaimed cans home for safekeeping because, as he told it, "you can't be too careful with tourists around." Madame Munoz, the butcher lady, remembered waiting tables during World War II for the Germans when they lived nearby. An American writer, Lisa Mann, lived in town with Bamboo, her cat. From what I could tell she gave away her manuscripts to other writers to use.

The Spender's house had a large living room with an Augustus John drawing and a James Whistler pen-and-ink sketch leaning on the mantel above the fireplace. A Henry Moore sculpture, all soft curves in bronze, sat on a long French farmhouse table. The kitchen was provisioned with Le Creuset enamel pots and Sabatier knives, big wooden chopping blocks and an iron pot rack. This was a kitchen equipped with a love of cookery and it was the place where I began my life-long love affair with preparing food. An expansive terrace faced the chalky hills of Les Alpilles, the little Alps. On either end of the house a flight of stairs led up to a bathroom and bedrooms, the children's rooms on one end and Stephen Spender's study with all its unpublished and first-edition manuscripts and the master bedroom at the other. The tiles in the children's bathroom were a stunning blue and white the Spender's had toted in their car from Italy. What they could not have known, since they didn't live there during winter, was how frigid those tiles were. Hot water flowed as a mere trickle from an instant hot water contraption hung on the wall and connected to a big butane cylinder below. The blue flame labored mightily but it was a losing battle. By the time the trickle met the big white tub it had lost its heat. Thus a bath was always a cold, hasty and nasty affair. We had come full circle, back to our unwashed days on the road in Scotland and Wales.

Despite the lovely food and wine and putting on extra layers of fat from all our cooking, the terrible cold of a "balmy winter" in Provence did us in. Once again we packed up the camper and hit the trail. This time I knew with certainty where we were going: we were headed home to the warmth of Spain.

MAKING *LIMONADA*

Heading Home to Spain

*You do well to weep like a woman for what you
could not defend as a man.*
— Sultana Ayelsha to her son, Boabdil, the last Sultan of Granada

Early in the spring of 1970, in flight from the icy gusts
of the Mistral we headed southwest to Spain. Under
a full moon we made a campfire beside the River Llo-
bregat as the lights of the monastery of Montserrat twinkled
high above us in the jagged outline of serrated mountains.
We were quite delirious to have found a quiet little road almost directly beneath an aerial tram that ascends breathtak-
ingly up the mountain. From our campsite a path led down
to the river where there were a few rustic tables, fire pits and
plenty of wood for gathering. On the opposite bank we could
see the occasional train passing from Barcelona, reminding
us we were not completely alone in what appeared to be a
lovely wilderness. I made fondue over an open fire, and af-
terwards, while Malcolm played his harmonica, we all sucked
on Valencia oranges, sinking into a drowsy torpor.

We had crossed the border from France a few days before
and immediately burned up one of the tires on the small

trailer we pulled, no doubt caused by our load of French cookware: iron crepe and omelet pans, a set of blue Le Crueset pots, and my hammered copper mixing bowl and whisks that I couldn't resist buying in a wonderful cooking store in Avignon. Malcolm good naturedly always seemed to find a spot for another treasure. Nestled in one corner was Lisa's violin, bought at an auction in Wales; tucked underneath was the set of Elizabeth David cookery books—sauce splashed and well used—that Natasha Spender had given me.

It was in this beautiful but isolated campsite that Lauren cried all night with an ear infection. In the morning we found a helpful farmer who directed us to the nearest *farmacia,* and the pharmacist sent us to a pediatrician who treated her very much like the children's doctor would have done in California. The farmer also sent us to a tire dealer who, in addition to selling us a new tire, recommended a local restaurant where we ate delicious Catalán shellfish paella while he changed the tire.

The Costa Brava was virtually deserted so early in the spring but the sun was brilliant and the beaches and coastline shimmered. It was all ours except for the occasional Spanish family and their picnics of chorizo sausages, olives, and loaves and loaves of bread. How could any one family eat so much bread? I wondered. One morning I bought a bag of crayfish and chunks of white fish at a local open-air market, packed our pans and a small stove down to the beach at Tossa del Mar, and cooked the crayfish in sea water that I scooped up when I waded out into the shallows of the Mediterranean. We slipped off their pink shells and doused those fat crayfish in the onion, garlic and olive oil in which I had cooked the fish. Voila! There on the beach our family feasted, sopping up the juices in the pan with crusty pieces of fresh bread. Two whole loaves we devoured. Now I understood those Spanish families and their bread.

We continued driving along the dazzling coastline, stopping to run around and play catch on the sand, parking alongside the beaches at night to sleep. A few nights we were awakened by a flashlight beam of light in our eyes from a pair of curious and watchful Guardía Civil on patrol. Then Malcolm had to groggily clamber into the driver's seat and find another more remote spot; once or twice the Guardía shrugged their shoulders and disappeared silently into the dark.

We explored what had been shepherd's caves that honeycombed a plateau near Spain's giant, blindingly white Sierra Nevada, still covered in snow above the city of Granada. Only one old shepherd remained and he seemed only too eager to talk with us and rushed inside his cave to rummage in an old chest for long-ago photos of a family from England who had once been his friends. And then we descended into Granada, fabled Granada. We found a room within the compound of the Alhambra that had a modern bathroom and oodles of hot water and thick towels. But the best part was a wrought iron balcony that offered a panorama of red tiled roofs and a raven's eye view of the street activity below. Children called up in Spanish to our kids who stuck their heads through the railings and kept calling down "*parlez-vous français?*" Early one morning a knife grinder on his bicycle passed beneath our balcony trilling a seductive melody on his flute. I lay in bed listening, thinking that the pipes of Pan must have sounded just like that; I had to squelch an almost uncontrollable urge to run after him. Horses hooves clip-clopping on the cobblestone streets below were soothing and hypnotic like a metronome.

From the city we ascended a narrow winding street and entered the Alhambra through the Gate of the Pomegranates; suddenly the clamor of the city fell away and we were in a cool woodland setting surrounded by the gurgles and trills of rushing water. Cascades of roses in full bloom, orange trees heavy with fruit, and bougainvillea, were a slash of crimson brilliance. Water rippled, flowed and shot playfully into the air from what seemed like a thousand fountains, their drops splitting into prisms and shards of rainbow-hued light. The enchanted Alhambra and the profligate gardens of the Generalife were ours to explore. We craned our necks at intricately carved ceilings, gazed at the views of the city below through filigreed arches, and were drawn on from courtyard to delicate courtyard as though sleep walkers meandering through a dream landscape. Yet for all its exquisite beauty, it was the crinkled faces of the ancient caretakers dozing on an old wooden bench in the Courtyard of the Lions that has stayed with me across the years.

After a few days in Granada we wound our way along the steep road that descends from the Sierra Nevada to the azure blue Mediterranean and the seaport provincial capital of Málaga, bathed as always in a glow of golden light. We were almost home. And an hour later we rolled into Fuengirola. "Hello again town," my heart called out. "I'm home. I feel like I never want to leave you again."

Concha the Walrus Dog

"I've got a present for you Mommy," she said
in the soft sounds of a three-year-old, while
clutching a red plastic workman's hardhat in her
young arms. And in its bottom, a fig, proud and
still warm from the tree.

— Lauren Celia Cohen

She wasn't much to look at with her bulging eyes and walrus shape. But she had fallen in love with our family and for her we were it.

We met her shortly after we first rolled into town in our red VW camper with the pop-top. We lived a block off the beach, in a small flat on the ground floor, directly across the street from the gracious old house and gardens—La Cancela—that had been our home before, so we knew the neighborhood well. The children could almost somersault out the front gate to play on the beach. One day a bulldozer came rumbling along the wide ivory stretch of sand, smoothing and leveling—a spring cleaning in preparation for the hot summer to come. All four children were down at the edge of the sand watching the work of this mammoth machine. Suddenly the roar of blades dropped to a steady hum. A few minutes later four sets of legs came running toward me where I stood keeping a watchful eye.

"Mom, there's this mother dog and her puppies in a nest she made in the sand and the man in the tractor was going to run them over and we made him stop and we got them out of the way…" Four sets of voices scrambled all over each other in shock at what had almost happened and excitement at discovering their own power. Then they set about finding homes for the puppies. Bravo to my kids. They spoke almost no Spanish, yet they managed to save this small family from being buried alive.

We took in one of her puppies, a little male, and named him Banjo. And each night, in the dead of night, his mother would come to our door to be with her puppy. How did I know? She had a thick tail that walloped the front door like a baseball bat. There was absolutely no way to sleep through the racket of her whacking the door, demanding to be let in. And so I did. At first it was to prevent her from waking up the landlady, who lived upstairs. And the kids did, and so the mother dog kept coming back night after night.

Banjo took to curling up under our van parked out on the street. One afternoon, I got in the car in a fit of anger over something or other, and drove away not even realizing I had driven over the sleeping puppy. And that night and the next and the next, the mother dog kept coming, but her puppy was no longer there.

A few weeks later we moved up into the *campo*—an area of big stucco homes, terracotta tiled roofs and adolescent lawns—where for the next month or so we lived in the guest quarters of an Argentinean writer, Carlos Thompson and his German actress wife, Lily Palmer. Malcolm had met Carlos Thompson in town at Bar La Cepa, and together the two men hatched a plan to go into business together, doing exactly what I wasn't sure.

In the Thompson-Palmer lodgings we had one room for the six of us and it soon became a chaotic mess of clothes, shoes and toys. Keeping order in a small space became strangely difficult after months of managing in our van. One morning I drove into town and rolled slowly past our old flat. I stopped at a stop sign intending to turn onto the main highway, the *carretera*, which cut through the center of town, when suddenly from the side of the van I heard an enormous racket: thump, thump, thumpety thump. There was no mistaking that sound and the tail delivering it. She had seen the car and she wanted in. And that was how Concha became our dog. And believe it or not, she joined us in the messy room at the big house on the hill.

MAKING *LIMONΛDΛ*

Bread, Clay and the Spanish Civil War

Each of us bears the imprint
Of a friend met along the way,
In each the trace of each.

— Primo Levi

P epe and his pottery yard were both ramshackle and to the casual passerby may have looked dilapidated, even unpleasantly cobwebby. All that is true I suppose, but the eyes that turned away after only a superficial glance would have missed a small, self-contained world, teeming with life and rich with history. The hub around which everything pivoted was Pepe himself, young and burnished bronze from the hours he spent muscling clay under the scorching Andalucian sun.

Discovering the pottery was like stumbling into a little community, revealed by my chance tumble down a dim corridor and out into the sun-drenched yard behind. I first saw Isabel, a roly-poly woman swaddled in an old apron, who lived in a few rooms that opened into the pottery yard.

"*Ven, ven,*" she called, beckoning me insistently with that characteristic Spanish imperative of fingers pointing down at the ground and a little scooping of the hand. So I ducked under her hanging sheets and ample underpants flapping in the Mediterranean breeze and found myself in the middle of a dusty yard of clay pots laid out on wooden planks, drying in the morning heat. Isabel had an incandescent smile and chestnut eyes that danced with so much hidden mischief that I would have followed her anywhere. At the time, due to my limited Spanish and her non-existent English, we communicated almost entirely by smiles and hand-signals. Even then I understood that the language barrier was a blessing. Since I couldn't talk much I could completely relax. I didn't have to say anything and didn't have to spin lies and false truths and didn't have anyone asking questions about my life in California, a life I pretended had never been. I could just get by on my smile.

Isabel was as staunch and sturdy as the trunk of one of the old olive trees that grew on the fringes of town. Her slight young husband rode a motorbike that made an eardrum-piercing racket when he fired it up. When I first met Isabel she was especially round, pregnant with her fourth child. Shortly before the baby was born her husband was killed in an accident, but I never knew how, since at the time I spoke about enough Spanish to ask for a drink of water. I did, however, understand the finality of the word "*muerto.*" The new baby, a second girl, was born with a wandering eye that gave her tiny face a sweetly skewed expression. And for a long while, Isabel, now wrapped in black, lost the magic of her smile. It never occurred to me to make the connection between her life and my own young husband's accidental death when I too was pregnant, since I was too busy forgetting and shoving my past into the shadows. But then Spain was the perfect place for hiding secrets.

The treasure of the place was Pepe. Pepe the Potter, as our family came to call him, to distinguish him from a whole town full of men called Pepe. On that first morning he was in his shed, seated on a board at ground level with his legs dangling in a pit below, spinning a mound of red clay. His smile was a sunbeam. The man was hospitable to kids and cats, fishermen who built boats in his yard, elderly señoras dressed in black who shuffled in wearing their bedroom slippers, seeking his advice or a hand with this or that. He was also kind to the Gypsies camped on the other side of the cinderblock wall that separated their world from the universe of the pottery.

"¡Hombre! Diana," he would exclaim with surprise when he would see me walk in through the dust after I too became one of the creatures who called the pottery home. If his hands were covered with the goo of wet clay, as they almost always were, he would invariably offer me his forearm to shake.

"¡Hombre! Diana." I can still hear him say it and know that I would be welcomed back no matter how long I had been gone. A few days, a few years, it was always the same smile of pleasure as he put down the cigarette glued to his lips—always a Ducado, the blackest of the black tobacco— and thrust out his arm.

If you closed your eyes and conjured up any figure, any shape, Pepe could quickly make it appear from the mound spinning between his fingers. Sometimes he'd have to cut it free to finish the details: the handles of a Greek urn or the ear-lobes of a Mayan mask, but the primary shape was always born there on his wheel. Once Pepe threw a long slender cylinder, then coiled it into a clay trumpet, finishing it with intricate scales and the head of a fish. That coiled clay trumpet hung in the hallway of our old house for years, until our time in Spain had run out. The man could make magic with his hands and a lump of clay he called *barro*.

The intricacies of glazing and painting fine designs eluded him however. If there is truly a goddess in the kiln during firing—potters will tell you that once the pots are in the kiln they're in the hands of the gods—those deities of glazing never did smile down on Pepe. Even the omnipresent ghosts of all the men who had worked at this pottery over the generations, loading and unloading the big kiln, were no help when it came to the glazing. Their spirits might still be lurking about, but what did they know of fancy glazes? This was a pottery that had produced the roof tiles for the Catholic church in the plaza, casserole dishes for preserving meat in salt when ice was still delivered on a cart by Salvador and his mule, Pepito, flowerpots and the two-handled coffee mugs called *pucheros*. This was a place that produced the utilitarian objects that people needed for their daily lives, not decorative pots with fancy glazes.

But Pepe was a dreamer. When I first became a regular, he was working with a young Parisian artist who had imported powdered glazes and was decorating Pepe's pots in the style of Italian *majolica*. When they opened the door of the big old white-domed kiln, after staying up all night shoveling debris and discarded wood into the flames below, they must have been seriously disappointed. The glazes had run and jumped spots and thoroughly misbehaved. It had to be discouraging to these two artists who had dreamed of making beautiful pottery to sell to the tourists who were starting to wander the streets. So Pepe was doomed to throwing endless flowerpots, ashtrays and casserole dishes and never did figure out how to fully express all his creativity. Yet his pottery yard remained the central address for anything made of red clay in the region, just as it had been for over a hundred years.

When I was at the pottery I could just be me, wordless and inarticulate. Nobody asked any more than that. I loved the silence and sitting and watching Pepe work. I loved the whole troop of people who called the pottery home: Isabel in her apron, watering her scarlet geraniums or hanging out her washing; Antonio, who could neither read nor write, building his fishing boat, using only a plane, a chisel and a hand saw. I can still hear his deeply sonorous voice as he announced his arrival each morning:

"Pepe, Pepe," until his friend's name floated like a particle of dust in the shafts of sunlight.

"*Voy, voy,*" Pepe would call back, hopping up from his place at the wheel to welcome his friend. I liked the ginger-colored cats that would sit around watching Pepe work. Between the fish heads and innards that Isabel tossed them each day when she cleaned fish for lunch and the detritus from the gypsy camp, they survived but had no trouble maintaining their sleek figures.

Afternoons and on Saturday mornings there might be one or more of our many young daughters, sometimes two or three of Pepe's—Celia, María José, and Montse perhaps, Isabel's two daughters, Isabel and MariCarmen, and my Lauren, playing together out in the yard.

"Mariquita," Pepe would sing out genially from his spot at the wheel, drawing out the "quita" like an opera diva holding a long trilling note. None of them were named Mariquita, but the girls heeded the warning nonetheless, knowing that Mariquita was the mythical naughty girl who had strayed too close to the clay pots drying in the sun. Especially in the afternoon sunlight they'd play around in the dust until Pepe finally swung the sagging wooden door of the shed shut and he and his girls would walk home in the dwindling twilight to Carmela and supper.

Celia, Montse, MariCarmen, Lauren and María José

After that first day I began going back, occasionally at the beginning and then almost every day and every free moment. I tried hard to visualize my hands and fingers working Pepe's magic with the clay. The cats and I would watch him sloshing around in the big pit where he dumped the raw clay and worked it using his bare, wide feet and the powerful muscles of his short brown legs. Every so often he would pull up a bucket of water from the old whitewashed well where the frogs lived amid the ferns, and throw the water into the pit, droplets of crystal scattering into the sunlight. Then he'd hop back in, stomping methodically back and forth until the mixture was smooth and the consistency of pancake batter. It would rest there in the pit for days while the sun sucked out its excess moisture. Then, when it had just the right consistency, he would carve it into big slabs, like cutting up a giant milk chocolate sheet cake.

By this time he had built a second potter's wheel for any aspiring potters-to-be, like me and another young woman from Italy who worked there at the beginning. Clearly he relished our company. He was also a patient teacher, especially when I had so much trouble mastering the art of the wheel. Those damp red lumps would wobble and tilt and were forever spinning off center. Still I stuck with it, perhaps more from cussed determination than anything else. And sometimes Pepe would throw a big cylinder of wet clay and hand it over for me to decorate. This I could do, and I'd lose myself in the work while he sat at his wheel smoking, spinning out ashtrays and casserole dishes and telling me stories of his boyhood growing up in the years following the Spanish Civil War.

Pepe was the magnifying lens through which I came to understand the town of Fuengirola and her history, especially the terrible years of hunger after the war. During the years I lived there and for many years after, the Spaniards were engaged in a collective pact of amnesia regarding anything having to do with their Civil War. Nobody said anything, not even in whispers. Except Pepe. Except to me. But I noticed how he always lowered his voice to avoid being overheard and risk being denounced to the fearful *Guardía Civil*. I started carrying a small notebook and ballpoint pen faithfully back and forth from our apartment to the pottery. On those clay smudged pages I would jot down the bones of his stories in Spanish so that I could capture their essence. By then I understood a fair amount but still spoke only meager Spanish, so I would often have to stop him to ask what a word meant. In that old notebook I recorded not only Pepe's stories but the stories his father had told him when he was a young boy, squatting in the dust, listening as his father too worked the clay.

"Diana," he would say, his voice dropping to a conspiratorial whisper, "there wasn't a dog or cat or even a songbird around for years. They either died from starvation or disappeared into some cooking pot. Even the rats and mice got eaten."

"I was born in 1932," he said, inhaling deeply as a big curl of cigarette ash dropped off the end of his Ducado. "Of course I have no memory of the beginning of the war in 1936. But my father always said that the three years of the war turned families, neighbors and even brothers against each other. He used to tell me how the German planes bombed our province of mostly poor *campesinos*—people whose only crime was trying to scratch a living from their small plots of land. So by early in the war Málaga was cut off from the rest of Spain. And that was just the beginning of the hunger. By the time the war was over and Franco's Nationalists had won, a third of the population was dead, disappeared, or had fled to France. That's what happened to Carmela's father: After the Nationalists and the Italians conquered Málaga, early in 1937, her father started walking toward France along with thousands of others who were fleeing. He kept right on going—he was afraid if he stayed that he'd be taken out at night by a Falangist death squad and shot. He never came back to live permanently with his family again. But the worst was yet to come." Pepe paused to light another Ducado, took a long drag and let the smoke out slowly.

"Meanwhile, the rest of the world, who had refused to aid the democratically elected Republic, and looked away when

Nazi Germany and Fascist Italy provided troops, tanks and planes to Franco's rebels, now had their own war, World War II. And who had time to remember the people in Spain?" He shrugged his shoulders and opened his damp hands with resignation. "Our animals were dead and the *fincas*, the farms, abandoned. There was no wheat to grind for flour and no bread. Many men and women had been killed or fled or they'd been rounded up and disappeared into prison. And the ones who were left, mostly the young and the very old, slowly starved. And the rest of the world forgot us.

"Diana,"—he always pronounced my name Deeana—"you have to understand that to a Spaniard, *es imposible comer sin pan*, a meal without bread is not a meal. Even if there had been food, which there wasn't, without bread it's as though we haven't eaten. By this time I was about ten, so I remember the Moor who would regularly come by boat from North Africa a few hours away across the Straits of Gibraltar, accompanied by his silent black bodyguard. He'd come to take back as much pottery as my father could make. At the time, money had no value since there was nothing to buy. My father would barter his *cerámica* for olive oil and sacks of flour and rice that would keep our family from starving. The next night my father would fire up the little clay oven—*el joven* Pepe, the young Pepe, he named it after me—and bake the bread late at night so the smell of baking bread would be carried out to sea rather than torture a hungry town. But early the next morning the women with their string bags and large, pleading eyes, were always waiting quietly at the gate.

"There were young women that dirt, hunger and despair had turned old, skinny women whose rags and sacks barely covered their naked bodies. There were gaunt babies perched on their mothers' bony hips with another silent child or two, their eyes oozing and their noses always yellow with snot, clutching her skirt hem. There were Gypsy women, spindly as sticks, young and old, but you couldn't tell the difference. Almost all the women wore black—*en luto*—mourning the husbands, fathers and brothers who'd died. With hopeless dark eyes and faces deeply lined from too much work, too much loss and too much hardship, they'd crowd at the gate of the pottery, hoping to trade a little salt or a few vegetables grown in the hard dirt, a couple of dried figs, or with nothing—*sin perder la esperanza*—hoping that my father would share a few bits of bread out of compassion for the children. And after the women had gone, my father was left with six loaves or so for our own family of eight: my father and mother, my five sisters and me, the youngest and only boy."

He reached out to the white clay *botijo* that was always sitting on the ground beside him and lifted it in the air. As he tilted his head back a thin gurgle of cool water arched elegantly out and into his open mouth. (When I tried drinking from this water jar I invariably splashed my chin and drenched the front of my shirt, to Pepe's frequent amusement. But I was getting better at it.)

He wiped his mouth and narrow mustache on the short sleeve of his shirt and picked up the thread of his story. "Hunger, deprivation and separation from their men left the women of our town vulnerable. My father once told me how the captain of the town's contingent of *Guardía Civil* treated the wives of the men he had imprisoned. When the women would come for a visit, perhaps bringing a small packet of food, the *jefe*—the chief—would force them to strip naked. He'd regularly rape the younger ones before he allowed them a visit." Pepe shook his head in what I understood to be beyond understanding. "*La mujer es un botín de guerra*," he said.

"Pepe, what does it mean, '*¿un botín de guerra*'?"

"Women are the spoils of war," he explained. "The cruelest way of punishing your enemy is to *violar* their women. Fuengirola wasn't the only town where this happened my father insisted, but in my opinion it's partly why people, to this day, hate and fear the *Guardía*. Diana, surely you've felt it yourself when the *Guardía* pass?" I nodded my head in mute agreement.

"*Mi padre* once told me how, despite the deprivation of those years, out in the *campo*—the countryside—the old orange trees continued to blossom and bear fruit abundantly. One day, underneath a tree, my father discovered the bodies of a man and woman whose guts had exploded from gorging on too much fruit."

At the beginning I had been drawn to the pottery by the challenge of mastering the potter's wheel, but now besides learning to use the wheel, I was absorbing both the language and Spain's history.

After listening to this story I understood why Spaniards of Pepe's generation were so short—in his case the top of his head may just have reached up to the tip of my nose. He seldom wore anything on his feet other than a pair of beat-up old sandals that he could slip in and out of with ease. He was bow-legged as though he had spent his life on the back of a horse rather than kicking a heavy wooden potter's wheel and he almost always wore holey old shorts that accentuated his sturdy legs. Whatever it was about him, however, whether it was his broad smile and unflappable disposition, his luminous dark eyes full of the delight of a child, or his generosity, always quick to share whatever he had, Pepe had some quality that drew people to him magnetically. He seemed enormously content with his place in the world despite his voracious curiosity about life beyond this village. Each of the assortment of people who found their way to the pottery seemed to expand the boundaries of Pepe's life. And irresistibly, we all fell in love with him, each in our own way.

La Cepa and the World of the *Extranjeros*

I hasten to laugh at everything, for fear of being obliged to weep.

— Beaumarchais

J ust like flowers, some people's personalities bloom with the light. I used to think of it as the refrigerator effect: the door opens, cold air rushes out, the light goes on, and the bloomers—I know this because I was married to one—do a two minute song and dance comedy routine. Perhaps it's because he's British. When Malcolm first went to work as a young salesman in London, his customers insisted he tell a few jokes before they discussed business. Or maybe it's because his mother played the piano in the theatre entertaining the British troops during World War II. He says he was practically born on the stage and that he and his brother were always waiting in the wings for their mum, Sylvia. She was 4 feet 9 inches tall and a true performer, the life of the party in any gathering, so Malcolm came by the refrigerator effect genetically you might say.

In those years, Bar La Cepa, on a corner diagonally opposite Fuengirola's plaza with its fountain and blooming geraniums, was the favorite hangout for all the *extranjeros* as the Spaniards called us. Foreigners. Yes, I suppose we were, although many had been residents in Spain for so many years they certainly didn't think of themselves as foreigners. And, by the time I discovered Pepe's pottery, I stopped thinking the word *extranjero* included me. That may have been one of the reasons I never felt I belonged at La Cepa.

The bar faced Nuestra Señora del Rosario Catholic Church with its green tiled roof, tiles that had been handmade years before by Pepe's father and his cadre of workers at the pottery a few blocks away. The church had been burned down in the first months of the Civil War, Pepe had confided. Then with a twig he had scratched 1945 in a piece of wet clay so he was sure I understood when the rebuilding was complete. I relished the fact that nobody at La Cepa knew about and probably had never been to Pepe's pottery, yet from the front of the bar you could have tossed a pebble over the rooftops and hit the pottery more or less.

By mid-morning La Cepa would be crowded and there wouldn't be a wobbly caned-top stool or tile-topped table left outside in the choicest spots for seeing and being seen. In the drowsy afternoons these tables would be filled with backgammon players, silently smoking, intently studying their boards. But in the morning this was the *extranjeros'* community center. By 11:30 a.m. jocular voices and raucous laughter would billow out the front door from inside where it was standing room only. "Have you heard the one…" would float out in the warm air. "Oh man, that's a good story"…followed by deep guffaws from throats crusty with cigarette crud. The light in the interior was dim and the empty beer glasses, white with foam, were already piling up along the wooden bar. From the front stools outside emanated more sedate discussions of life in New York, American and British politics and other bits of the expat community staying connected to each other and the world beyond the village. Even the *extranjeros* understood in some wordless way that in Franco's Spain you absolutely didn't risk talking about Spanish politics, even in a foreign language. One never knew who was eavesdropping.

They were a motley group, the La Cepa regulars. There were the retired couples, many from New York and the East Coast of the U.S. who would migrate farther east at the beginning of winter and stay for the warmth and the relaxed way of life, departing each spring, just after Passover. It didn't hurt that social security checks and U.K. pension schemes bought more leisure and comfort here in southern Spain than just about anywhere else in Europe. There were also the British colonials who, although Africa was no longer their home, still wore khaki shirts and knee-length shorts as though they were about to depart on safari. They would describe their gracious estates, pampered lives and adventures in the bush. "By Jove we shot for the pot," they'd boast in their booming voices of their big game encounters, while the sweat splashed down their florid cheeks. And they would continue to gnash their teeth in innocent bewilderment, trying to work out with anyone and everyone who would listen, why "the bloody natives had been so ungrateful."

Malcolm was in his element among the La Cepa crowd. With his talent for mimicking ethnic voices and his large repertoire of jokes, he was always the center of some hearty crowd of laughing regulars. His gregarious personality craved an audience and it didn't hurt that he understood the thrust and parry of quick repartee. I, on the other hand, was hopeless. I never knew what to say. I tried hard enough but it was a strain and I felt like a fish flapping around out of water, drowning in the air. I was usually thinking of clay pots…not exactly the stuff of witty conversation. Thus I'd shift my weight miserably from one foot to the other and count the seconds until I could slip away unnoticed. I envied Malcolm's social ease and imagined him practicing his song and dance routine at night, alone in the kitchen in the glow of the refrigerator light bulb.

He used to tell me about the contingent of "remittance men" who hung out at La Cepa, men whose families sent them a monthly remittance to stay away from wherever it was they originally hailed from. For example, there was Eddie Gay, "by name and not association," he hastily asserted when introduced. It was his stock line. I first met Eddie Gay and his perennially askew toupee, when a red Jaguar convertible with its top down slowed to a crawl at my heels as I walked home to lunch one day from the pottery.

"Do you know who I am?" sang out a plumy voice, as though I most certainly should. The tanned middle-aged man wearing a cravat at the neckline of his shirt looked as though he might possibly start to weep as I shook my head and walked on, barely pausing to notice.

Eddie had amazing timing and would bang the big black iron door knocker in the shape of a fist that sent echoes somersaulting along the tile floors of our old house.

"Ah…Eddie…we're just sitting down to lunch," Malcolm would say.

"Oh terribly sorry old chap…I won't stay long," he'd respond, slipping like mercury through the barely open door.

"Hello Eddie," I'd call in greeting. "Can I offer you some lunch?"

"Oh heavens dear girl, I couldn't eat a thing. I've just finished. Mmmm that smells lovely. Perhaps just a small taste." And suddenly we had Eddie Gay for lunch seated at our table out under the banana and castor trees in the patio.

He wasn't a bad sort really, just a bit needy and certainly more than a bit lonely. Malcolm relished retelling the mishaps of Eddie Gay. Like the time Eddie asked a man to move saying, "Excuse me but you're standing in my sun." Or the lively tidbit involving an altercation at La Cepa between Eddie and another man which ended when the taller chap reached over, snatched aloft the toupee, spat into it, then smacked the hairpiece back in place. That snazzy red Jaguar convertible could not prevent loneliness in a town like Fuengirola where half the expat community seemed to keep themselves just sufficiently topped up with high-octane spirits that they could never feel their feelings.

Some of my favorite people were ones you never saw at La Cepa. Winifred Lownes, a widow in her 70s, lived with style and grace in a faux Spanish village, Pueblo Mijas, a fifteen-minute walk from the plaza. Winifred's youthful spirit became part of our extended family and she filled the role of grandmother, albeit a hip and trendy one. One morning she joined us for a drive in the countryside, out to see the land we'd bought where we hoped to one day build a house. At the time the back roads were no more than deeply pitted donkey tracks so that you ended up galloping along on a very rough ride. While crossing the river, swollen after recent rains, our van stalled in the middle. Soon foaming brown water began seeping under the doors. Undaunted lady that she was, Winifred simply rolled up her trousers and followed us, stepping into the muddy swirl, wading her way to high ground without a murmur of complaint. She would occasionally fly home to Málaga from the U.S. on the pink Playboy jet, a perk afforded her as the mother of Hugh Heffner's business partner in Playboy Enterprises. Once or twice Winifred brought home an exhausted Playmate of the Year who needed a little Spanish village R&R.

If Winifred was a grandmother to us, Percy and Alice Seitlin, who were La Cepa regulars, became surrogate parents for the ones I'd never had. They were retired and split their year between Fuengirola and Greenwich Village, New York. Percy, whose life had revolved around the New York publishing world, affectionately called me "Mrs. Dearly." "Be happy," he'd tell me. "Not slap happy, just happy." Over the years he read drafts of my stories. "I know you'll get it right," he'd jot in the margin. "You have a good, true voice." Alice wore her gray hair in a braid wound tightly around her head and let Percy take the lead telling stories. Sometimes I'd ride the train with them into Málaga on warm winter afternoons to hear a concert by one of the visiting European orchestras. I'd take my camera, a roll or two of black and white film, and photograph the aristocratic old buildings as the three of us wandered around the city admiring the architectural details. Then we'd sashay confidently into the stately Málaga Palacio Hotel a short walk from Calle Larios, the main street, to sink into the leather sofas and chairs in the lobby and have a rest before heading off for the music. As we walked Percy and Alice would talk to me about their favorite composers and about Vienna when Percy was psychoanalyzed by a protégé of Sigmund Freud. Percy would tell me stories of the round-table luncheons at New York's Algonquin Hotel and the world of writers and poets, his world. Alice's universe was one of music and composers, New York's New College, and Alberta Hunter singing jazz at The Cookery. They gave me glimpses into a world of the intellect, a world I hungered for but could not have named. And I, for my part, gave them creative family dinners gathered around the old wooden table ablaze with candles in our patio. I'd find something at the market that inspired me to do some serious cooking. Then Marshall would ride his bicycle a few blocks over to their apartment on the Paseo Marítimo with an invitation to join us for dinner. We lived in a world without telephones so spontaneity ruled. The Seitlins always said yes. Percy was a grand raconteur and Alice kept him straight on the details. "No Percy, that's not how it went," she'd admonish him, like any comfortable partnership of many years. We shared multiple Passover Seders with the Seitlins and they came with the children and me to Morocco to visit our friends the Bensimons. Percy and Alice were always up for one of my adventures.

Málaga as we knew it

Our neighbors across the street were the writer John Gordon Davis and his wife, Patzi. They had both grown up in Rhodesia and ended up living and working in Hong Kong, where they met. John was a larger-than-life character and his boundless energy filled a room with its power. He spent his days cocooned with his typewriter on the second floor of their house, writing, always writing, and emerging like a disheveled nocturnal beast, only after dark. By the early 1970s he already had five novels published. Whenever I saw John he invariably had an open amber bottle of San Miguel beer in one hand and a lit cigarette in the other. Patzi had straight blond hair that she was always pushing back behind her ears, an infectious laugh, and once composed "An Ode to a Rissole" as a thank you for some croquettes I'd made and carried over to their house. We became fast friends and once took our daughters—Patzi's Shirley Anne and my Lauren— both the same age, to Morocco, where we stayed in some flea-infested cheap hotel, and got bed-bug bites all over our faces. Everything seemed funny when I was with Patzi, especially as we gazed at each other's bug blemished faces.

John's booming voice and laughter exploded with such force that he'd rock back on the rear legs of our rather rickety rush-caned chairs, until I worried that he might topple over. He told us wonderful stories of his life in Africa, describing how he'd driven back and forth across the continent with his writing table strapped to the top of his van. While doing research for *Taller Than Trees*, he accompanied the hunters patrolling the tseste fly free zone circling South Africa. Any animal, including the large game animals that strayed inside that perimeter, was shot on sight. For another book, *Operation Rhino*, he worked rounding up and relocating the black rhino, one of the most dangerous creatures on earth, to save them from extinction by poachers. As a coda to his tales of adventure he'd dissolve in cascades of laughter, like cymbals crashing in a grand finale of sound.

It may have been Winifred who introduced us to LaVeta McCosh, a retired clothing designer from New York. La Veta too became a special friend of our family. She lived a block away from us in one of the old Spanish houses that she had remodeled to accommodate her large design studio. I particularly loved a mosaic patio that she had made from tile bits collected from all the gracious old houses that were being torn down all over town to build apartment blocks. The village as I first knew it was starting to disappear but the change was so gradual that it had yet to become blatantly apparent, although I'm certain La Veta noticed, since she never missed a detail or any opportunity to find old treasures. That marvelous mosaic floor was an example of her infinitely creative imagination. She could fashion anything from denim and leather and designed tennis clothes for Australian Lew Hoad's tennis club on the road to Mijas. For a time she also worked with Malcolm, refashioning used jeans when he opened his denim and candle shop called La Llama, The Flame, next to our house. La Veta smoked constantly and her deeply husky laugh came freely but I wasn't always sure what she found so funny. I just smiled and hoped it seemed like I got it too, whatever "it" was. She also made magic with plants: her various patios on the many levels of her house brimmed with stag horn ferns, their gray-green fronds arching handsomely, and it is from La Veta that I came to love them. Flowering begonias overflowed baskets tucked in shady corners, lilies cascaded from Asian pots and all manner of other growing things were tucked in here and there; I thought her house was like an arboretum before I even knew what an arboretum was. It was never too much but just enough to suggest the luxuriant insouciance of nature fully ripe. La Veta shared her life with Margaret, a tiny round, elderly lady always dressed in pink but we never could figure out their relationship. LaVeta was clearly the creative force and out-going personality of the two while Margaret just faded into the background like old wallpaper

"You'll never guess who's coming to dinner," Malcolm announced one afternoon. I had no idea. "Stan Getz and his wife, Monica," he said, sounding very pleased with himself. I'm sure I knew the name because I loved Bossa Nova but per-haps not that he played the tenor sax. That night the four of us sat outdoors eating tapas at a small bar around the corner from our apartment. Stan and Monica were easy to talk to and seemed to really enjoy this thoroughly new experience of an unpretentious bar and the wonderful food it served. Over the years we would see Stan from time to time when they were on the Costa del Sol for a long holiday. Malcolm would describe the scene at La Cepa when Stan, who had stopped by for coffee, would raise his hand for the waiter and half a dozen people, as Malcolm told it, would hop to their feet to help. Such were the perks of being famous. Several times our David had a sleepover with the Getz's son Nicky.

A few early mornings Stan came knocking on our door, and I'd take him out riding on Lisa's horse, Manolete.

"I wrote a song for my father," he said one morning as we ambled along on the horses. "I'm still working out the ending but I'll play you what I've recorded so far next time you and Malcolm come by." Another morning he surprised me by saying, "I've never learned to read music…oh I can read it enough to get by but I don't really read it. I just know the notes in my head." We'd trot along for an hour or so until the morning Manolete's saddle slipped and Stan tumbled off. At the time it didn't appear he'd hurt himself, but by the time he reached home he had an enormous hematoma on his leg. That was the end of our riding excursions. His system was so badly damaged by years of drug abuse that the slightest bruise could turn into a bloody mess.

MAKING *LIMONADA*

The Damaged-Pet Shop

*St. Thomas says you cannot love a horse because
it cannot love you back. This statement proved a
serious obstacle to my entering the Holy Roman
Church in 1948.*
— Penelope Chetwode, *Two Middle-Aged Ladies in Andalusia*

Neither Lisa nor I had a shred of common sense
when it came to the discarded animals we brought
home because we were too soft hearted to turn our
backs on them. Over time we all ended up referring to our
house as the damaged pet shop. I think it was Malcolm who
laughingly first called it that name. And at the beginning it
was funny.

In our earliest mishap we bought the children the sweetest
yellow chicks at an open-air market one Sunday. First Lauren,
who was still an unsteady toddler, ran across the lawn after
one of the chicks, stumbled and fell, making a chick pancake.
Then the three survivors, who were by then adolescent hens
and roosters-to-be with all their white pin feathers starting
to come in, slipped into the house when we were gone one
afternoon. It's hard to imagine that a few young chickens can

do so much damage but it looked like a hurricane had blown the barnyard full force indoors; fluff and feathers were on every surface, shredded plants and chicken poop smeared, pooled and tracked everywhere. I can't say that it made me fond of those chickens. Their days were numbered and they quickly ended up in Carmela's stew pot, three fresh, tender young chickens for Pepe's family. I can only guess at what a paella and chicken *cocido* Carmela made with them.

Some months later, after we had moved for the fifth time to a second floor apartment up the street from the pottery, I won Hurdy Gurdy by tossing *cinco duro* coins into a glass plate at a fair. He was a day-old bit of golden fluff, a downy Pekin duckling that imprinted on me, as newly hatched ducklings do. Hurdy Gurdy followed me everywhere; I was his mother duck. He grew into a handsome, snowy-white fellow with a small feather curl at the end of his tail; he had bright yellow webbed-feet and a broad orange beak. He was allowed into the apartment because the floors were marble and I could just wipe up after he did a wee squirt. Hurdy Gurdy was like a second dog and Concha, gentle soul that she was, didn't mind him at all. He would waddle into Lauren's bedroom at night while we told the children bedtime stories. He'd settle down in a little mound of white feathers between the beds and chortle duck sounds of contentment while Concha would be curled up in a circle nearby. The whole family would snuggle comfortably on the two twin beds with their iron head- and footboards and mattresses that sagged like old swayback horses. We took turns reading, Malcolm and I, and if we didn't read we'd make up a story. Many nights I would recite from my childhood memories:

How Many Miles To Baby land?
Why anyone can tell.
Up one flight and to the right
Please to ring the bell.

Hurdy Gurdy heads to market

And I'd sing "A Roundup Lullaby"—the coyotes yipping skeerie, just singing to his dearie…" an old cowboy ballad by Badger Clark that I had learned around the campfire as a Girl Scout. Or I'd trill toura-loura-loura, an Irish lullaby. Hurdy Gurdy was just another one of the kids loving story time. Before we turned off the lights I would scoop him up and stash him out on the deck under a large terracotta flowerpot. I don't know where I got that bright idea, but he didn't seem any the worse for it. I can still hear the unmistakable sound of his muffled quacks coming through the porous clay walls of that big pot.

One morning as I was walking back from the *mercado* I saw our red VW camper with Malcolm and the kids flying off down the *carretera*, the main road through town. What I didn't know was that they were a duck ambulance, taking an injured Hurdy Gurdy to the vet with a broken leg. He had flown off our balcony and landed two floors down in the street. As Malcolm told it, the vet just shrugged his shoulders and suggested,

"*¡Cometelo!* Just eat him." Indeed. I've always been inventive so I tore up to the *farmacia* in the plaza, slipping in just as it was closing at 1:30. I bought plaster-of-Paris to make a cast and tape. Using the dining room table as an operating theatre, Malcolm and I splinted his leg with popsicle sticks and put a plaster cast around it while it healed. Until I took off the popsicle sticks many weeks later, Hurdy Gurdy had a comical, lop-sided waddle. The leg healed perfectly.

Meanwhile the passengers on the ark began to arrive: Sam, a vivacious raven-haired beauty, the wife of a Canadian film director whom Malcolm and I had come to know very slightly through Carlos Thompson, out of the blue, offered me her shiny black, four-year-old Arab stallion, Arés, when she and her husband returned to Canada the following month. I could barely believe she meant it. My own horse: a dream come true.

Marshall and Hurdy Gurdy

Although I had ridden horses when I was ten years old, it was only as often as I could earn enough money selling greeting cards door-to-door to pay for an hour or two on a droopy rental horse at Sleepy Hollow stables. I was the daughter of a single mother who struggled to buy food and pay rent. Own a horse? Hardly, but horses filled my dreams and my heart. I was a beautiful, wild white stallion who whinnied shrilly and cantered freely across the mesas and meadows of the sweetest dreams of a young girl.

Then I grew up and went to live in Spain. Even then I never in my wildest imaginings thought I would ever have a horse of my own.

Arés was actually hell waiting to explode. The last bit of advice Sam gave me was that I had to have him gelded before he would be safe for me to ride. The process was barbaric. A group of stable hands tied his front and back legs together and somehow wrestled him to the ground. Without anesthetic, someone, certainly not a vet, took a big pair of loppers and chopped off his testicles. The horse screamed. It was brutal. I was sickened, but I forced myself to stand and watch and accept responsibility.

I was so deliriously happy to have Arés that I didn't have the good sense to be afraid to ride him. I'd never saddled or bridled a horse by myself before, but somehow I figured out how to cinch up my tiny English pigskin saddle and slip the snaffle bit between his teeth. Fear never entered my mind. But even after he was gelded, Arés would take it into his head to go plunging down the side of a steep cliff without warning and no amount of tugging on his gentle bit would get him to slow down. So it was "Sally bar the door" sort of riding…good for learning how to stay in the saddle but hard on my heart.

Arés

It was equally unnerving to ride him through the narrow streets of town out into the countryside. Young men would zip up behind us and toot the shrill horns of their small autos or their motorbikes, calling out *piropos*—flirty remarks—intended to distract me or spook the horse. Granted it was probably the first time that anyone had seen a young blond woman riding her handsome ebony horse through town, not quite Lady Godiva, but unusual. The men thought they were funny or cute, but it was really annoying. And it was scary since Arés was quite high-strung.

Pepe, Malcolm and I built a small stable back behind the big dome-shaped kiln at the pottery. We constructed it of large concrete blocks cemented together. The cement ate away the skin on my fingers. The stable wasn't a thing of beauty but the work was a labor of love. Outside, we made a small corral where Arés could stand looking over the wall into the cluttered detritus of the gypsy camp, or out to sea, the breeze off the Mediterranean like a lover's breath, riffling his blue-black mane.

In the winter when he developed a cough I carried a small blue propane stove down to his stable and heated an old bucket filled with water from the well. I dumped in Bay laurel leaves until the steam rose up in mentholated clouds. Then I held a blanket over his head, and stuck my own under as well to keep him company. I babied that horse with love and care, yet one day as I was putting alfalfa in his manger, sweet-talking him all the while, he whipped his big beautiful head around and bit me on the top of mine. He could be one mean *hombre*, but he was sure a looker.

Sometimes the children and I would climb the stairs to the roof of our apartment where we had an unobstructed view of Arés out in his little paddock. We'd shout his name over the red-tiled rooftops to see if he would look our way and recognize the sounds of our voices. I would have happily moved him into our second story apartment if that had been an option, but having him just down the street at Pepe's pottery was plenty good enough.

I rode him that fall in Fuengirola's annual *feria*, a festival of horse parades, music and dancing that goes on night and day for a week. As the clattering hooves of the horses made their way along the sea front I sat tall and proud in my tiny English saddle, heels down, so proud and thrilled that I thought my heart might explode. About this time we bought Lisa an older, gentle white gelding named Manolete. Lisa looked lovely on her white horse, her blond hair tied back with a black ribbon; a black *sombrero* Cordobes and ruffled white shirt completed her riding attire.

Malcolm and Lauren riding in the feria

One sunny Sunday while out for a drive exploring the *campo* we spied a white English sow and her eleven piglets. Forgotten and forlorn on the outskirts of the litter was the smallest, the runt, who had lost the end of his tail because, the farmer explained, his mother had sat on him. (At least we think that's what he said.) The tiny piglet's problem was immediately apparent: too many siblings, not enough faucets. So in my meager Spanish I pleaded with the farmer to let us take and raise him. Lisa named him Frodo for the character in *The Hobbit*, her then favorite book. And Frodo joined Concha and Hurdy Gurdy and our family of six in the second-story flat. It seemed perfectly logical to me that the best place for Frodo was the fireplace in the living room, which is where he lived for the first month. Finally our maid Antonia, who took excellent care of our apartment and of us, drew a line in the sand: either the piglet had to go or she would.

So Frodo joined Arés and went to live at Pepe's pottery. Pepe built him a pen and Carmela brought the leftovers from their mid-day meal each afternoon. That lucky piglet regularly feasted on Carmela's golden paella and all the uneaten bounty from her kitchen. In a land of good cooks, Carmela was more than a star, she was a constellation. Fortunate little pig. Slowly the pink and white piglet grew into a handsome, portly fellow who often came out of his pen to roam around in the dust when Pepe didn't have any pots drying in the sun. Afternoons the pig would snort happily around Arés's hooves, raising little dust clouds with his breath; Arés would drop his head and snuff Frodo's bristly back, but otherwise just ignored him. I would often see Carmela and Pepe, heads together, admiring Frodo's growing girth. I should have been savvy enough to realize that all this doting on the pig would come to an unwelcome end, but I was blissfully unaware of any larger scheme in Pepe and Carmela's minds. It was so obvious: What family in Spain keeps a pet pig into old age?

Diana, Isabel, Lisa, Lauren and María José with Frodo

MAKING *LIMONADA*

Desayuno and the Blind *Mula*

Garlic (ajo). The spice of Spanish life.
— Janet Mendel, *Cooking in Spain*

Pepe's mother Isabel was a tiny wisp of a woman, brittle as a dry branch. In the manner of Spanish widows she always dressed in black, with a diaphanous black scarf floating about her head. By the time I knew her, Pepe's father had been dead for years. She still lived with several of Pepe's unmarried sisters in the small white-washed cottage on *Calle España*, a few blocks from the pottery, where all six of her children had been born. A robust Canary Island date palm grew in the center of her patio and towered over the cottages of her neighbors. Golden bunches of dates grew high amidst the palm's arching fronds, mute testament to the health of the tree. A few years later, when a bulldozer came to clear the site for an apartment block, the old cottage collapsed quietly in a cloud of stucco and dust, but that old palm put up a real fight. I stood out in the street silently rooting for the tree.

Mid-morning, from my seat at the potter's wheel in Pepe's workshop, I would hear his mother's voice, soft as a whispered prayer: "Pepe…Pepe." I'd hear too the faint footfalls of her black slippers on the hard-packed earth. A moment later her small dark frame would project the skinniest shadow across the sunlit doorway. In one hand she always carried a ceramic bowl covered with an embroidered napkin, and in the other, a red earthenware mug with two handles called a *puchero*. Her arrival was Pepe's signal to heave himself up from the pit where he had been throwing pots, go out to the well for a battered bucket of water to splash himself clean, and have his *desayuno*, his breakfast.

"¿*Quieres comer?* Want to eat?" he'd ask, and without waiting for my answer, he'd motion me to where he sat and place the mug in my hands and hand me the choicest piece of grilled bread, oozing with olive oil and fragrant with garlic. The robust flavors would hit the center of my brain while the aroma swirled up my nose. It was not a breakfast for the delicate palate. In the *puchero* was *café con leche*, hot and sweet, flecked with yellow dots of oil from the milk. Other mornings the bowl held *churros*— crisp-fried curls of dough that we dipped into the coffee—tucked beneath the embroidered napkin to keep them warm.

I was walking past his mother's open doorway one morning and sang out my greeting. "*Buenos días Señora.*"

"Diana, *ven*," she croaked, motioning me into her tiny kitchen where she was preparing her only son's breakfast, grilling the thick slices of rough bread over a small charcoal fire. When the slices were crusty, branded with diagonal grill marks, she rubbed each slice with a clove of garlic, sprinkled them with a bit of coarse sea salt, then smashed them with the palm of her frail hand into a plate of dark green olive oil. "I love your *pan tostado con ajo y aceite*," I told her. I'm certain Pepe's mother, who I respectfully called Señora, could tell from my broad smile that this was so. She nestled the slices into a clay bowl, covered them with a napkin, and then poured hot milk into the *puchero* of coffee. Instead of thanking her and walking on ahead, I accompanied her that morning down to the pottery, slowing my pace to match hers. I felt rather honored when she allowed me to carry the clay bowl of grilled toast. We didn't talk much but I enjoyed her companionable silence.

After his mother left, Pepe and I sat in the open doorway of the pottery, sunlight streaming in a shaft, heavy with flecks of golden dust. We ate the toast and shared the *puchero* of coffee back and forth. I saw his mouth and chin glisten with the fragrant oil while my own mouth was exploding with a thousand points of pleasure. Just as on other mornings, the perfect time for Pepe to tell me a story about his boyhood was when he was eating his breakfast. In those years Pepe carried his father's breakfast down to the pottery, just as his mother did now. He didn't say it, but I knew that the ritual "*¿quieres comer?*" and sharing the *pan tostado* and *puchero* of *café* was something he and his father had done hundreds of times across the years.

He told me how he used to squat in the dust next to the spinning mound of clay and how his father would hold his small hands lightly around it so he could develop a feel for when the clay was spinning centered and true.

"Saint's days and holidays were the best in my memory," he told me me after taking another swallow of *café*. "Then I didn't have to think about school and my professor with two thumbs on his left hand. 'Cano you oak tree,' he'd thunder to my indifferent sums, and thump me hard on the head with his ruler. I didn't like him or his school, up a flight of narrow stairs, so I always tried to find excuses. But my father insisted I learn to read and write and not be *un analfabeto*, illiterate.

"Have I told you the story my father told me of Juan, the miller, who ground the wheat and flour for the town's bread? This was before the Civil War. There wasn't much to eat, but there was always bread, so grinding the wheat for bread made Juan an important person." Pepe carefully wiped the oil from his mustache and chin with the linen napkin. "Everyone in Fuengirola knew Juan and his mule. The grain was ground on a big round stone around which the mule walked steadily, pulling another big stone that reduced the hard kernels of wheat into flour. Juan's mule was growing old and tired— nearing retirement you might say." Pepe's eyes crinkled with mirth. "One day Juan bought a young *mula*—a female—to raise and train her to pull the heavy grinding stone. He didn't realize it when he bought her, but the *mula* had been born blind. And, by the time he noticed he'd grown so fond of her that he couldn't think of parting with her. My father used to laugh and say that although Juan the Miller had three sturdy sons and two bright-eyed daughters, the young *mula* was clearly his favorite.

"As it happened the *mula* was so intelligent that she didn't need eyes; she had a sweet, willing disposition and was devoted to Juan. In the hot afternoons of summer, when they had finished work for the day, Juan would take the *mula* down to the beach for a swim in the cool Mediterranean. He never needed to tie a rope on her; she was always loose and walked about freely, always at his side or following closely at his heels.

"One Sunday morning Juan had taken the *mula* down to the beach for her morning swim. Juan himself didn't swim, but he used to roll up his trousers and wade out into the shallows with the *mula* by his side. Where the water got deep enough she would just sink in and start to swim, but she always stuck pretty close to Juan. But this particular morning the *mula* apparently lost her sense of direction and by the time Juan realized what was happening, she was already drifting beyond the rocks that marked the end of the bathing beach. Soon she was no longer able to hear his voice. She was swimming in large circles and was slowly being carried out to sea."

Like any good storyteller, Pepe knew the most riveting spot to pause. He reached into the pocket of his shirt hanging on the old, weather-beaten door, and grabbed the blue and white package of Ducados and his matches. He stuck one unfiltered cigarette in his mouth, ripped the wooden match against the corrugated doorframe, then sucked deeply as the cigarette tip glowed red. Not in any hurry, he let the smoke out slowly through pursed lips, savoring the taste, or so it seemed.

"So Juan began frantically yelling for help," he continued. '*Socorro...socorro*,' Juan yelled. Fortunately it was a warm morning and there were already many people lolling about on the warm sand and paddling about in the water. People started gathering in an excited crowd around Juan who was pointing out to sea and calling '*Socorro...socorro*.' You could just make out the *mula*'s dark form against the brightness of the water. Suddenly the crowd sprang into action: a few brave bathers bolted into deep water and began flailing in the direction of the mula. Several others grabbed a small rowboat, dragged it to the water, hopped in, and began rowing energetically toward the *pobre criatura*—the poor creature. Even the few fishermen, who had been laying out their nets to be mended on the sand, pushed off in their larger boat, started the motor and headed out to the small, dark head, faintly visible from the beach. Soon there was a small flotilla of flailing arms and an assortment of boats bobbing about in the water, making their way to save Juan's *mula*.

When they reached the exhausted animal they gently guided her back using their voices to urge her on and their paddles to keep her headed in the right direction. There were so many small craft on either side of her that my father said it looked like a summer festival. Meanwhile Juan had waded out as far as he could safely go and his voice called to her above the voices of the excited crowd. As the bedraggled creature made her way up onto the sand, cheers and applause erupted and groups of people began congratulating each other with hearty slaps on the back, big grins, and lots of handshaking for a job well done. And Juan was so happy to have his *mula* safely back on the beach that he called out *"Vamos, ¡una copita para celebrar!'* and he invited everyone to join him for a drink at the local bar.

"Vale," Pepe said, ending his story using the same flourish as Cervantes had ended Don Quijote. He ground his cigarette stub out with the heel of his sandal and nimbly dropped down onto the board at ground level and resumed kicking the heavy wooden wheel with his wide, calloused feet.

At times lanky Antonio, one of the town's fishermen, would build a boat out in the dusty yard of the pottery, using only hand tools: a saw, a carpenter's plane and a chisel, to cut and shape the staves. He braided and rolled by hand long sinewy snakes of rope that he prodded and pounded between the planks to prevent leaks using a big wooden mallet. "Thwonk, thwonk," was the song that mallet sang. I'm pretty sure Antonio didn't know how to read or write well, if at all, but he built solid, sea-worthy fishing boats, always painting the finished hull a lively color, and almost always naming her María. Of all the people who would come and go regularly, Antonio was my favorite and once in a while, after I too became one of the regulars, Pepe would have his mother prepare the three of us one of her special dishes for lunch. About 2 o'clock, after she'd brought the still bubbling food and a fresh loaf of bread, Pepe would gather up a few of the *cazuela* dishes that were stacked here and there, splash them free of dust with water from the well, wash himself clean and offer us a bucket to wash in. He'd produce a few small amber bottles of San Miguel beer and three battered old forks that he kept for such grand picnics. We'd dig into the pot communally—each spearing a piece of meat or fish with our forks and dipping our bread in to sop up the sauce of whatever succulent stew his mother had prepared. Sitting there in the sunlight with these two old friends in companionable contentment, the world around us dropped away. I was a part of their small town, Spanish universe. I felt utterly happy.

MAKING *LIMONADA*

Carmela

You don't want to hear the story
of my life, and anyway
I don't want to tell it, I want to listen
to the enormous waterfalls of the sun.
                            — Mary Oliver, Dream Work

W as it my passion for her paella or my passion for her husband that inextricably tied Carmela and me together? Food and love—the most primal of needs, and they both tangled messily in our friendship.

At the beginning we were an unlikely pair of friends, Carmela and I, at least that's what I thought at the time. In 1960s Spain, Francisco Franco and the Catholic Church decreed that a woman's place was at home birthing babies and caring for her husband and aging parents. There were few other options for women in Andalucía. When we first met in the doorway of Pepe's pottery, we were both in our twenties. Carmela had already borne Pepe five dark-eyed daughters: Isabel, the eldest, named for Pepe's mother, MariCarmen, named for Carmela's mother, Célia, María José and Monteserrat, called "Montse" who was a chubby toddler, about the age of my Lauren. And that was before José

Antonio, named for his father and his grandfather, was born and then Rebecca, a few years later. Carmela also cooked, cleaned and struggled to earn a few extra *pesetas* here and there to supplement the modest sums of money Pepe earned by selling his flowerpots, ashtrays and earthenware casseroles. Mornings she and her mother would sit in front of the central market and sell shellfish on a damp burlap sack. And if they didn't sell it all they could always take it home and Carmela would cook it for lunch. Work and having babies—that was pretty much the extent of Carmela's life as I saw it.

Then my family and I wandered into their lives: blond, blue eyed and California free. And Pepe? Well, he was hospitable. Like Carmela, I also had children, two sons and two daughters, but I still managed to spend half my day up to my elbows in clay, laughing and talking, hanging out with her husband and writing down the stories he told me.

I had a *criada*, a young woman who came six days a week to cook and clean, so I had lots of time to be off riding my horse, working at the pottery, or having an adventure, and for the next few years the adventure was often with Pepe, Carmela's husband.

Pepe became my pal, my best friend. I didn't intend to fall in love with him, but fall under his lovable spell I did, just like all the other endless characters that called his pottery "home." In addition to making room for Arés's stable and Frodo's pen, Pepe was an endlessly patient tutor in my labored efforts to master the potter's wheel. He also became a friend to my husband and someone dearly loved by my children. We just sort of melted into each other's lives. Of course nobody asked Carmela if this was O.K. with her. It was just the way it was, and I think she loved Pepe so much she would never have said, "Stop, enough!" Or if she did, I never knew.

Don't get the impression that Carmela was weak: she had a tough, shoot from the hip style, and no patience for fools. Still, she tolerated me and my frequent presence at her husband's pottery. Once in a while when she'd walk in and find me there and very little work underway, she'd give me a dark look and a barely courteous,

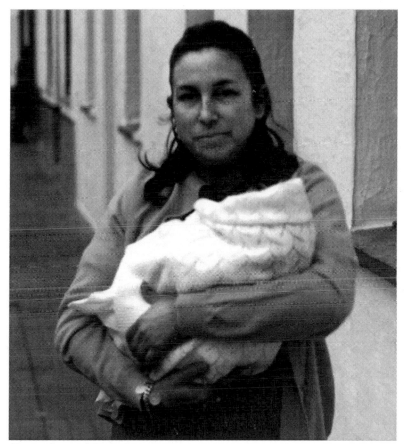

Carmela and José Antonio

"*Hola*, Diana." The resentment in her tone was withering. Yet Carmela and Malcolm figured out how to put up with each family spilling over into the other's life. Carmela and Pepe even asked us to become the godparents for their newest and sixth child, their only son, José Antonio. The fact that we were Jewish seemed unimportant.

On the 19th of March we were invited to their four-room fisherman's cottage to celebrate Pepe's name day, *el día de* San José. In her tiny kitchen Carmela lovingly prepared Pepe's favorite dishes: chicken *en pepitoria*, braised in white wine, ground almonds and garlic and *ensaladilla rusa*, a mounded potato salad with home-made mayonnaise and tiny pink shrimp. I stood at Carmela's elbow and watched her beat egg yolks with a fork until they were thick lemon cream, then she let me hold the *aceite de oliva* bottle aloft and drizzle in green oil in a fine stream while she whipped furiously. On some Sundays, the two families with our collective nine children would pile into our VW van and head out along the river for a picnic. Pepe and Malcolm would make a wood fire and Carmela would cook shellfish paella in a big iron pan balanced over the fire on large rocks. She came on these picnics in her housedress, her feet in worn sandals and her legs swollen with varicose veins; she'd bend over the hot flames to gently stir the bubbling broth and keep the rice from sticking. Sitting around in a big circle on the dusty ground, we'd devour heaping plates of golden rice until all that was left were empty clamshells and piles of pink shrimp tails. After she made coffee over the dying embers, Pepe and I would take whichever of the kids who wanted to go off for a hike, while Malcolm threw a ball around with the others and Carmela stretched out her weary legs for a well-deserved rest. In those days I loved Carmela's food, especially her paella, more than I loved Carmela.

At times the four of us would head into Málaga in our van to attend a parade or the *feria* and drive back in the dark, with Malcolm and me singing two-part harmonies at the top of our lungs in the front seat—"You are my sunshine, my only sunshine…" Carmela and Pepe would nod smilingly from the back, his arm thrown affectionately around her shoulders.

On occasion they came to our apartment for a game of cards. I'd serve something to eat, probably something American style since I still wasn't much of a Spanish cook, but Carmela couldn't quite hide her dislike for what she considered to be "foreign" food; once or twice I caught her rolling her eyes.

At the time Pepe completely eclipsed Carmela in my affections. He was the one with the great sense of humor, the artist, the philosopher, and the storyteller. Carmela was Pepe's wife and the mother of their *familia numerosa*. She was an enviable cook, someone whose skills I wanted to emulate in my own kitchen, and she was a no-nonsense, hard working, loyal and patient wife. Period.

MAKING *LIMONADA*

Estrella

Knowing me in my soul the very same—
One who would die to spare you touch of ill!
Will you not grant to old affection's claim
The hand of friendship down Life's
sunless hill?

— Thomas Hardy

Sssaape…sssaape," hissed the plump woman dressed in black as Concha and I walked past one morning on our way to the pottery. "Buenos días, señora," I called cheerfully so she would understand the dog was with me. She gave me a curt nod and mumbled *"buen día"* of greeting and shook her twig broom menacingly in Concha's direction to scare her away. Concha was fairly plump herself and looked about as scary as a stuffed toy.

"*Buenos días* Pepe," I announced as I stepped out of the sunlight and into the cool interior of the pottery shed. Barely waiting for him to reply I blurted out, "Why do all the women grab at their skirts and press back against the walls and hiss 'ssape…ssape…' whenever a dog walks past." It was a warm Monday morning and I could see the small beads of sweat that had already formed along his brow.

"*¡Muy buenas!,*" he responded with a grin. "Ah, Diana," he said taking a deep drag on his omnipresent Ducado, letting the smoke out slowly. I could tell that this question would be answered by a story or an anecdote and Pepe was just gathering his thoughts on where to begin. He was seated at his usual spot, down at floor level, legs dangling down in the pit where he was kicking the wooden wheel. This morning he was making ashtrays, dozens and dozens of ashtrays.

"For so many years after the Civil War there wasn't much to eat and the only animals in town were usually sick or the dogs were rabid," he explained, using *hidrofobia*, an unfamiliar word. "*¿Que quiere decir hidrofobia?*" I inquired without hearing the similarity to English.

"*¿No lo sabes que quiere decir rabia?*" he asked rephrasing the question. "Ah…*rabia. Si claro que lo entiendes,*" he continued when the light bulb of recognition registered on my face. "Haven't I told you the story of Estrella?" I shook my head.

"I'm sure I've told you how every morning before school, I used to bring my father his *desayuno* here at the pottery. On one of those mornings—I must have been about eight at the time—I was heading home to pick up my books when I saw a small boney puppy shivering in the thin sunlight, huddled beside a freshly scrubbed doorstep. He looked so sad that without thinking, I bent down and scooped him into the empty earthenware *puchero* I was carrying that had held my father's coffee. Without another thought for school and my two-thumbed professor with his head-thumping ruler, I hurried home.

"As the youngest of six and the long prayed for *niño* after five girls, I was hugged, kissed and indulged by my entire family. So even though my mother's eyes got big when she saw what I carried in the *puchero*, she nodded her head, wiped her hands on her apron and found a piece of rag to wipe off the coffee and sugar that stuck to the puppy's panting sides. Then she took pieces of bread from her drawstring bread bag, soaked them in a little water and gave them to him on a saucer. He was so small that at first he didn't even know what to do. Diana, you need to remember that we had just survived the Spanish Civil War so there wasn't much to eat. Wasting food on a dog wasn't something a family could do.

"I remember my mother's thin shoulders in her black dress hunched over the small puppy. I think it was the first time I realized that I had never seen her wear anything but black and also saw how gentle she was with animals. So letting me keep the puppy without any protest wasn't really a surprise. Although till then, the only animals we kept were chickens and once a year my mother raised a pig out in the yard here at the pottery. When my sisters came home for lunch they squealed in alarm at the skinny puppy.

"'*Mamá,*' whined Antonia, my oldest sister. '*Por favor mamá, no dejes que ese animal se quede en casa…vamos a tener pulgas y bichos*…please don't let him keep that buggy animal in our house…' she pleaded, working herself into fake tears. But our mother just smiled and said we'd wait to see what my father said. And when my father came through the door for lunch, he said '*bien, está bien.*' So I named the puppy 'Estrella' which means star in Spanish, and Estrella became just another member of our family of eight.

"Days later the angry owner marched into my father's pottery and demanded the dog back. My father, who was always a genial man, apologized for my having taken the puppy.

"'Amigo he said, 'let's go have a coffee.' And off they went to the corner bar with my father's arm conspiratorially around the other man's shoulders. After a *café*, a talk about this and that, and almost certainly a small shot of anis, my father asked him if he was willing to part with the puppy for, say *cinco duros*, which at the time a man might possibly hope to earn as a few day's wages. A while later they came back chatting amiably, then parted with a handshake and Estrella became truly mine."

Pepe finished the last of the ashtrays he'd been forming on the wheel. Now every board, splayed like spokes on a wheel around where he sat, was filled with the glistening wet shapes. He swung himself up off his seat and began carrying the loaded boards out into the sunlight where they'd dry before he fired them in the big whitewashed kiln. When he'd finished he came back into the dim shed, turned his back on me and began to knead a large slab of red clay.

"Bueno, ¿y qué pasó?" I asked with interest. Pepe picked up the story exactly where he'd left off.

"Estrella began to put on weight and lose the shriveled puppy look. Always hungry, he'd wolf down the remainder of my mother's saffron-hued paella from our Sunday lunch, leaving only the tiny clam shells behind. He ate scraps of bread soaked in broth, garbanzo beans, leftover lentil stew, fish heads and scaly chicken legs. Whatever else that remained from our table—there was never very much—was divided up for Estrella and the pig. My mother had an old round, three-legged black pressure cooker that she'd fill with yellow chicken feet that she'd sometimes find tossed away at the butchers. After she'd finished cooking for the family, she'd nestle the pot full of chicken feet and water in the hot coals and leave it to cook with its small black top-knob hissing back and forth, until those ugly feet had become mush and the water was a soupy gelatin. Estrella loved this mess and he'd eat until his sides ballooned out like that funny old black cooker.

"I filled a burlap sack with straw, slid it under my bed, and that's where Estrella slept. I used to laugh because he'd yelp and whine as though he was chasing cats in his dreams. He was like my shadow; he came with me to the pottery each morning when I delivered my father's breakfast. And he was waiting for me when school was over and all the boys exploded out the door towards their houses. Most of them were a bit in awe of the two of us, because at the time, if people kept dogs, it was only to tie them up as watch animals. They couldn't walk around freely and never came in the house. But my friends started to like Estrella's daily vigils outside our professor's house. They'd play with him but when they got too rough, Estrella would give a low rumbly sort of growl, letting them know he'd had enough. He didn't bother much with my sisters who never quite lost their fear and awkwardness with him. Even today, stories of the wild dogs, ravaging in the mountains of the Sierra de Ronda make the women afraid of even brushing against a dog. And that's why they hiss.

"In the evening Estrella would lie with his head resting on his tawny paws, waiting for the sound of my father's sandals. As the door would swing open Estrella would bound forward and stand up on his hind legs and put his front paws on my father's shoulders and they'd stand that way for a few moments. By now Estrella had grown into a large, solid, salt and pepper colored dog with large chestnut flecked eyes. A little like the color of Concha," he nodded toward where she dozed sprawled outside in the shade thrown by the corrugated roofs.

"On the hot afternoons of summer," he continued, striking a match along the rough board where he sat and lighting a Ducado, "when even the Mediterranean was lazy and only the flies moved, we'd lie side by side, Estrella and I, stretched out on the cool tile floors of my house. I'd day-dream about sailing a fishing boat to North Africa or having a bicycle to ride down the coast to Málaga.

"On winter days my sisters and their friends would gather at our round table in the front room to gossip and crochet. Even with their legs tucked safely under the heavy tablecloth that hung to the floor keeping in the heat from the charcoal brazier of coals underneath—*la mesa camilla*—some of the girls would still perch on the sides of their chairs. They kept as far away as possible from Estrella who was sleeping peacefully on the floor. Sometimes when those girls would break into cascades of laughter and little shrieks, Estrella would open his eyes, regard them soberly as though he was considering their foolishness, groan and go back to sleep.

"Leaving the pottery one morning after sharing my father's breakfast, I got as far as the well where the turtle lived when I realized that Estrella wasn't with me. Turning, I saw him stretched out amid the rows of casseroles drying in the sun. I called his name but he only lifted his head, thumped his tail in the dust agreeably and went back to sleep. For the first time he stayed behind and I walked to school alone.

"Later my father told me what happened. About mid-day he was out in the yard bending over a large pot filled with silver blue lead glaze. He said he was stripped to the waist, his arms blue to above the elbows from dipping and swirling the pots in the thick glaze. Suddenly he heard high-pitched screeches of alarmed women filtering in from the street.

Estrella lifted his nose in the air sniffing and all the short hairs along his back rose to stiff bristles.

"Through the short passage from the street lurched a snarling, dirty dog, covered in phlegm, with its jaws snapping like a child's wind-up toy. The dog headed straight for my father. He said that as he jumped to his feet, glaze and casseroles slopping across the ground, Estrella leapt forward with his teeth bared straight at the intruder. The fight was ugly, he told me, the two dogs matched evenly in size and rage. A cloud of dust and howls filled the air, until Estrella tore open the throat of the other dog which ran bleeding into the street and dropped in a limp pile of mangled fur. Estrella had a large tear wound on the nape of his neck. Hanging his head in pain he limped off dripping blood, heading home.

"When I got back from school he was in his usual place under my bed, but no coaxing or calling would get him to come out. He'd just whimper and tremble in response to my calls. My father went to find one of the local *Civiles*—there was one who knew a little about animal medicine. The *Guardía* came to the house in his stained green uniform and removing his black patent-leather hat, he bowed formally to my mother, and followed us into my room. Then he listened to my father's story. We pulled the heavy iron bedstead out from the wall and the old Guardía, his hands carefully folded safely behind his back, bent over Estrella curled on his sack.

"I remember it seemed like time had stopped. He shook his head and told us to tie Estrella out in the patio, and if over the next few days he started to be fearful of water that would be a sign he had rabies. *Rabia,* the word scared me. That's what all the women who clutched their skirts and all the stories of mad dogs in the Sierra de Ronda were about. So we tied Estrella under the big palm tree in our patio. He turned his back on us as though somehow he was ashamed. I lay in bed that night and the next nights making promises to God if he would only see this thing with Estrella my way.

"But Estrella wouldn't eat or drink and within days he was alternately snarling and yelping at the bowl of water my father had placed under the tree. I only went out to him once; he got very quiet and looked at me sadly with his large amber eyes.

"The *Guardia* came again. Poor fat bellied man had one of the few guns in town. With slightly unsteady hands he pulled a parcel wrapped in a cloth from inside his wide leather belt, carefully unwrapped it, aimed and fired. I don't know what happened. I don't know if he was just a bad shot or if seeing me with Estrella since he was a puppy...I just don't know. But he emptied his gun slowly, shot after shot into the dog's body, and still didn't hit a mortal spot. Estrella just lay there under the palm tree, slowly bleeding to death in the dust.

"In the evening I got the burlap sack from under my bed and emptied out the straw. My father pushed Estrella's body into the sack and I can still hear the heavy thud it made as it slipped over the doorstep onto the street as he dragged it off. Our house seemed very quiet for a while. We never had another dog."

"*Lo siento*, Pepe," I murmured, since I didn't know what else to say.

The Ineffable World of Naphtali Bensimon

"I am not averse to women's education," a liberal
sayyid told me… "so long as it is not excessive. If
it is carried on to the age of nine and then stops, I
do not think it can do any harm."
— Freya Stark, *A Winter In Arabia*

The gritty port city of Algeciras, down the coast toward Gibraltar about an hour and a half by car, was
the embarkation point for what would become many
family adventures. This time we had lurched across the
churning gray Atlantic, through the Straits of Gibraltar, on
the great old ferry *Ibn Battuta*, from Algeciras to the dazzling
white port city of Tangier, Morocco. It was blustery and cold
during the crossing and our family of six had huddled together out on deck to keep from being seasick. After disembark-
ing, we waved off the swarm of young touts who clustered
around us like flies on decomposing fruit, climbed narrow
stairways and scooted through dank alleys up to the ancient
city that literally hung above us. This was North Africa, and
we may well have stared. Most of the women were veiled and

wore headscarves to cover their hair; all wore *chilabas*—caftans that secreted their bodies to below the ankles. Most of their feet looked calloused and as worn as their cheap plastic sandals. The men, too, were cloaked in *chilabas*, their faces hidden in the shadows of their hoods. They padded along noiselessly in pointy-toed, backless leather slippers. The older men wore tasseled scarlet fez perched on their heads. Nobody made eye contact with us and nobody smiled. Clearly we weren't in Europe anymore.

We vaguely understood that because of anti-Semitism, most Moroccan Jews had fled to Paris or Israel but we were curious to see what remained of the once vibrant Jewish community. Malcolm asked in creaky French for the *synagoga* and someone waved us to one of the few remaining old synagogues. That's where we first met Solomon Bensimon, a tall young man who looked about nineteen. At least we thought he was about nineteen, for when later we asked his age, he was a bit vague. We were inside the synagogue, peering around when Solomon's slender frame appeared out of the shadows. He had a faint little mustache above his upper lip, and he very sweetly engaged us in conversation in almost perfect English. I had never seen a Sephardic synagogue. Ornate silver lamps hung suspended like stalactites from the ceiling. There was a stuffy balcony up a tiny stairway, where the women sat during services, screened off and unseen from the men downstairs. This was the Orthodox Sephardic way.

During this first visit, the *shamas*—the synagogue's caretaker—showed us some of the treasures that remained, treasures he was now hoping to sell to wealthy Jewish tourists so they wouldn't languish in a dying community. Besides, he and the congregation—what was left of it anyway—needed the money. We bought an old *megillah*—an old parchment scroll coiled around a hand-carved dowel hand-lettered in Hebrew that recounted the story of Purim and the Jews in ancient Persia.

Solomon Bensimon

We also bought a large brass tray with Hebrew letters hammered by hand on its surface. I was seduced by an ivory silk embroidered shawl with long knotted fringes, but we couldn't afford it. (Once in a while I think about that shawl, recalling the weight of the silk, and hope it now drapes over beautiful shoulders somewhere else in the world.)

Solomon seemed starved for conversation and invited us around the corner to meet his family. That's where we first met his father, Naphtali, his silent, perennially smiling mother, Coty, his younger sister, Tamo, and little brother, Josef. That's how it all started, as simply as that. Little did I know then that our lives would become intertwined and that the Bensimons would play an important part in my personal history.

Tamo was a roly-poly sixteen, with large, dark eyes full of the innocence and wonder of a child in a developing woman's body.

"Retarded," Naphtali spat as introduction, with a mixture of humor and scorn playing about his large face. As I was to discover, Tamo spoke English, Spanish, French and Arabic; she loved disassembling anything electronic and complicated: cameras, radios, games. Then she'd put them back together again, perfectly. Portly little Josef was nine and clearly his father's joy. The only times I ever saw Naphtali's ferocious eyes lose their stern expression was when he gazed adoringly at Josef.

And, after that first encounter, the children and I, mostly Marshall and Lauren, would often return, sometimes for one of the Jewish holidays and sometimes just for the pleasure and adventure of the place and the chance to be part of the Bensimon family. The first Passover our family shared with the Bensimons, two rotund Moroccan women were seated on low stools in the kitchen, bent over aluminum pots on the floor, peeling mountains of carrots. How could any one family use that many carrots for even a dozen holidays? I wondered. It was such a small detail but it didn't make sense.

Each time we returned for a visit we were welcomed joyously, like cousins. We would stay in a rag-tag cheap hotel close to the Bensimon's apartment, and in the mornings, Coty, Joseph, Tamo and sometimes Solomon along with Lauren and Marshall and I would all traipse off to the open air fruit and vegetable market, alive with bundles of green mint, perfect mounds of golden lemons, charcoal braziers with skewers of lamb and chicken grilling that sent clouds of pungent smoke billowing up in the warm air. Then on we'd go, following in Coty's footsteps like ducklings, to the spice market where the slanting sunlight was a deep golden haze from the mountains of turmeric, cinnamon and saffron.

The children and I ate wonderfully fragrant food in little stalls and wandered the narrow alleyways of Tangier like family, always accompanied by giggling Tamo and mischievous little Josef, and often Solomon too. As we passed tiny restaurants and tea houses, minor-key music, so endlessly repetitive to our Western ears would pour out, the wail of the singer's voice almost indistinguishable from the wail of the stringed instruments. I came to love that music.

Yet I cannot forget the morning we were happily ambling along together in a dim street so narrow that the fragile wooden balconies of the old apartments above us, both right and left, were so close they almost touched. That morning a young man wearing a *chilaba*, the details of his face lost in the shadowed folds of its hood, hissed "Juif" as he passed. Jew. He might as well have spat on us. My first encounter of being the despised "other" robbed me of my idyllic innocence; I never felt fully at ease walking those streets again. Yet I never thought to ask Naphtali or Solomon what it felt like for them as Moroccan Jews, to love your country yet know you were unwelcome.

There were oddities and shifting, shadowy peculiarities not only in the city of Tangier but also within the family. Almost every time we came to visit, the Bensimons lived in a different flat. They moved multiple times even within months. Asking why would have felt intrusive, so I didn't.

Veiled women, slumped mutely in rickety, paint-chipped chairs were a fixture in the entry of all their apartments. Slunk deep into their ankle-length caftans, cheap rayon scarves covering their heads and hair, the women seemed to possess infinite patience. Or was it resignation that I saw in their sagging shoulders? Sometimes it seemed like they sat there for hours and that time had simply stopped on the Jewish Orthodox Bensimon side of the threshold.

Solomon was often sent abruptly dashing off to destinations unknown on errands for his father. They were a Jewish family in a hostile Moslem country, yet Solomon didn't have a life of his own, even within the tattered remnants of the Jewish community. He seemed to have neither friends nor fun—except for playing tour guide to my children and me as we ambled the streets and alleyways. Beyond that, he hovered in the apartment waiting to do his father's errands. What were these mysterious errands? I never asked the question. Maybe I was so enthralled with the enchantment of it all that I didn't want to see any deeper. Or just maybe I picked up on some unspoken rule that you didn't ask probing questions that might bring out uncomfortable answers.

Sometimes Solomon had to deliver his father's directives: "Diana, don't sit on his bed if you're …umm…unclean." The words stumbled out of his mouth in obvious discomfort. I had smacked up against the prejudices of being female in an Orthodox Jewish world.

Early on, in perhaps the only time Naphtali touched me, he swooped up my palm and stared intently at its lines and creases.

"Yours will be a long and healthy life," he said. "You will have another husband and another child."

It was one of the few times over the years that I knew him that he had engaged me in direct conversation. His broad smile beaming down from his great height and girth suggested he had presented me with a golden gift. Some gift. To me it felt like he had just deposited a large dead rat in my lap. Clearly he didn't understand that I was only thirty, already on husband number two and had four children. Four. What the Spaniards called a *"familia numerosa."* But in the circumscribed world of Orthodox Judaism sandwiched between the "women should be little seen and not at all heard" restricted world of Moslem Morocco, having husbands and bearing children was the pinnacle of life. Like so much of what my twentieth century eyes saw in Tangier and the Bensimon world, it seemed arcane.

There was another woman in the Bensimon family, Naphtali's old maiden sister Zohra, who, like Coty, was only a shadowy presence. We had never exchanged more than faint smiles but one day she drew me aside. Peering up at me through bottle-thick, black-framed spectacles that magnified the intensity of her raven eyes, she motioned for me to lean in close and confided in a wispy voice, "My brother and I have the blood of our great-grandfather, the great Jewish mystic Solomon ben Simon. His gift of seeing the future runs in our blood." She showed me the underside of her skinny wrist and prominent blue veins to make sure I understood. She then lit a candle and set it afloat in a saucer of water. Slowly a subtle rainbow of colors began to drift on the water's surface. She bent her head so that her glasses almost touched the edge of the dish, her gray hair so dangerously close to the candle's flame that I almost grabbed her bony shoulder to pull her back. But that touch would have seemed too intimate and I didn't.

"You will do well in your life," she whispered. "God will guide you on a long and difficult journey."

At least this explained why all those silent women sat so patiently at the Bensimon threshold. They had come to learn their future.

Naphtali reading Lauren's palm

Bicycles, Friendship and *Chumbos*

*...the keen, unpassioned beauty of a great
machine.*

— Rupert Brooke

It was already the sort of summer morning when the heat
shimmied on the asphalt and the glare off the whitewashed cottages made me squint. Pepe and I had just
polished off the last crumbs of his mother's *pan tostado* and
café; I could feel the perspiration beading on my forehead
and I hadn't even started kicking the heavy wheel. I'd ridden
my new *bicicleta plegable* to the pottery that morning to show
it to Pepe. Folding bicycles had become quite popular since
they could be stashed in small living spaces, which is how
most Spanish families lived, multi-generations piled lovingly
on top of each other. I had showed Pepe how a hinge on
the bicycle's main down tube opened and allowed the front
wheel to completely fold over the back.

Given the sweltering temperatures, I opted to work that
morning on a large cylindrical sculpture of a Mayan funeral
mask that I had slowly been developing over the past weeks:

large disc earrings, stylized gaping mouth with curving incisors…it held promise of being a striking piece…if I didn't make a mistake.

"*¿Cuando eras joven tuviste una bicicleta?* Pepe," I asked after I'd settled into my work and he was again seated at his wheel. Today it was flowerpots that filled the wooden planks. "Did you have a bicycle when you were young?" I'd never seen any of Pepe's five daughters riding a bicycle so I wasn't sure that having one was such a big part of being a kid here in Spain as it was when I was growing up in California.

"*Claro que sí*, Diana," murmured Pepe. I glanced up from carving away extra clay from my sculpture to see him nodding his head affirmatively. "Most of my friends had bicycles before I did. Sometimes they'd let me ride around town—I learned to ride with one of my friends running along behind me as I wobbled down the *paseo*—or one of them would give me a ride on the back of his bicycle when we rode out to the *campo*. But I longed for a bicycle of my own. Finally I persuaded my mother that she should talk my father into buying me a bicycle." He paused to brush his arm across his forehead where the sweat was glistening.

"One day when my father went to Málaga, he bought an old bicycle, he called it an antique. I think he paid something like 250 pesetas for it. In the city of Málaga there wasn't another like it. In all of our province of Málaga there probably wasn't another. The bicycle was red and a BCA made in Italy. My father thought that the most logical way it came to be in Málaga was that an Italian soldier brought the bicycle to Spain during the Civil War. You remember, don't you, that Italy sent soldiers, food and planes to support Franco? Between Italy and Germany, the Nationalist rebels had everything they needed while the Republic begged the world for help and received nothing." I could hear the bitter tone of injustice in his voice. "And probably, my father thought, the bicycle got left behind when the soldier returned to Italy. If he was lucky enough to make it home," Pepe added.

"I was about 12 years old at the time, but I wasn't very tall. So my father fastened blocks of wood to the pedals so that I could reach them. I rode that bicycle for about a year and a half until one day I was out riding with a friend and I broke a piece of the fly wheel. In those days the flywheel was made in one piece. I pushed that bicycle around to all the workshops in town. I was hopeful that it could be repaired but nobody had a part. Then my father took it to workshops in Málaga but it was impossible to fix as no replacement parts existed.

"Meanwhile, my father and mother had decided to buy me a new one. One morning before school—it was just a regular day—as usual I brought my father's breakfast down to the pottery. He had placed the new bicycle in the door-way, still wrapped in its paper from the *tienda*. I walked in here but didn't pay attention to the package leaning against the door and my father didn't want to say anything. But as I turned to leave I saw blue and red stripes visible through the wrapping paper, and an unmistakable shape of wheels, handlebars and a seat. I thought the bicycle was for me but at the same time I couldn't quite believe it. Then I looked at my father's face and the faces of the other men who worked here and they were all grinning at me. Then I knew it was for me. I was so happy. I think I even rode it that first day with some of the wrapping paper still attached. That was a day I had more important things to do than go to school or even eat. I proudly showed off my new bicycle to all my friends and to all the people I passed in the street and I gave my friends rides on the back. To test the tires I rode the bumpy road into the *campo*, down to Los Boliches and along the river to the castle.

"A year or so later my friends and I began riding into Málaga; it took us about two hours to get there, riding hard all the way. We'd also head west along the old road to Marbella and Estepona. Once in a while, on a Sunday, I'd rent my bicycle for 3 *pesetas* an hour or 25 *pesetas* for the whole day." Pepe paused to wipe his wet hands on his shorts, tapped out a Ducado from the clay smeared package, struck a match deftly on his wooden seat and sucked in the smoke..

"One summer two friends and I even rode beyond Málaga. Somewhere along the way I had a disagreement with one of them, and we didn't talk to each other for the rest of the day. Meanwhile we lost track of the hour and by the time we turned around we had to ride back to Fuengirola in the dark. It was already late as we were passing Torremolinos; then I got a flat tire. We didn't have tools or a pump with us and everything was closed. After we walked several kilometers the third friend left to ride home to Fuengirola so he could tell our families. But the friend with whom I'd had the argument stayed with me because he didn't want to leave me alone. Then he had an idea: With a piece of wire that we found along the road we pried off the tire and pulled out the tube. Then we yanked up dried weeds growing along the roadside and stuffed them into the tire. When we had packed the tire full we pushed it back onto the rim and that's how my friend and I rode home. For coming home so late and worrying my mother, my father said I couldn't ride my bicycle for a week.

"I had that bicycle until I was probably 30 years old; I never wanted to sell it. One day I passed a *campesino*, walking into town along the old *carretera de* Coín. I'd seen him many times before; he was always bent almost double carrying a load of wood on his back. I brought him here to the pottery and gave him my bicycle." Pepe flashed me one of his twenty-four carat grins, signaling he was finished with story telling and ready to move on. He flicked away what remained of his cigarette and wiped his hands on his shorts.

"*Ven conmigo* Diana. Come on, I want to show you something," he said hopping up agilely from the wheel. I followed him out into the sun burnt yard—even Concha was sprawled out panting in the shade—and back along the long wall that separated the pottery from the Gypsy camp.

The wall was about six feet high and made of the same gray blocks of cement as the work shed. In a number of places the old blocks had tumbled down and lethal prickly pear cactus had grown up in their place, forming an impenetrable barrier. The large oval pads of the cactus were covered with tiny tufts of almost invisible golden spikes that would burrow painfully into unsuspecting flesh if you were silly or distracted enough to brush against them. By now, in late June, their fruit—*chumbos*—was swollen like large, rosy colored eggs. I watched as Pepe hacked off a long pole of *caña* that grew at the back edge of the yard, and cut one end into a three-pronged fork, then hooked the ripest *chumbos* and yanked them to the ground.

"I roll them in sand to remove most of the spines, like this," he said as he squatted in the sandy dirt. He grabbed a stick to prod them with. "I tumble them around, like so. It's how my father taught me," he explained as he speared one fat *chumbo* with a knife and with another knife sliced off both ends of the thick rind and with a neat slice down the middle, peeled back the outer covering. "Now you can grab it without fear of stickers." I reached in and took a bite of the watermelon colored fruit; not quite as juicy as watermelon, yet with a similar sweetness and texture.

When Pepe had accumulated a mound of the fruit, he headed over to the well and drew up a bucket of icy water and dropped the unskinned *chumbos* in to chill. At two o'clock when he headed home to lunch, he carried the bucket of fruit home for Carmela, her mother, their five daughters and their young son, José Antonio, our Godson.

Shriveled Gypsy women would sit outside the central *mercado* with mounds of *chumbos*, plucked from the other side of Pepe's fence, displayed at their feet. A few days later I remarked to him that the Gypsies were selling his *chumbos* but he just smiled and said, *"hay bastante para todo el mundo,"* there are plenty for all.

If you pressed *cinco duros*, a twenty-five peseta coin with its stern profile of Francisco Franco, into the Gypsy woman's boney palm, she'd slice down through the rind, then you could reach in and grab the fruit to check its sweetness without fear of prickles in your fingers or even worse, in your tongue. The rest you could carry home in a cone of newsprint. Just like Pepe and Carmela's family, our family came to love those *chumbos*.

Favorito

...and in the dream he rode the sun steed of his future...this horse, named Herzhorn, which has wind in his belly and snuffs the sun stands in the stable and gladdens the boy's heart.

— Sophocles, *Oedipus*

A year or two after Arés dropped into my life came another fluke: A Dutch artist, Job Birker, who had lived in Spain for most of his adult life, couldn't return some money we had lent him and offered me his dappled white Cartujano stallion, Favorito, as a way of repaying his debt. And there I was with two brilliant horses where before there had been just daydreams—young horses with gorgeous conformation, thick necks, long, glossy manes and abundant tails—spirited horses as opposite in temperament as their colors.

Unlike Arés's unpredictable fire, Favorito had a noble and dignified spirit. I'll never forget riding him the first time: he was a luxury race car with acceleration like silk and huge reserves of power. The Cartujanos are the progenitors of the Lipizzaner horses of the Spanish Riding School in Vienna. With both Arés and Favorito, it took most of my free time to keep them exercised and ridden properly. Then, after a while, it became clear that I had really given my heart to Favorito. Yet how could I possibly part with Arés, the horse I had dreamed of owning since the time I was a girl? I stewed and agonized over what to do. Nobody could help me; I had to work it through for myself. Fortunately a young American couple that I knew through a yoga class owned horses that they cared for in their own stables. They were crazy about Arés. Still, when I sold him, I left the check they had given me sitting on top of the refrigerator, un-cashed for weeks. Cashing it was the final step that I couldn't quite take. Finally, without telling me, Malcolm signed my name— forged it really—and deposited it in the bank. I realized the check was no longer where I had put it and asked Malcolm if he had seen it. He seemed honestly baffled by why I would be upset. I felt deeply angry that he didn't respect my feelings or my boundaries.

I fell in love with Favorito the way young mothers fall in love with their babies. I would stroke his silken hide and run my hands along his belly, exploring him with the fingertips of a lover. I'd lace my arms around his muscled neck and bury my nose in his white mane, inhaling his musk. I had toppled heart-first into a love affair with another sentient being. I would have happily taken care of him but by this time I was spending less time at the pottery, so I boarded him where we boarded Manolete, at the stables of Pepe the Horse up beyond the bullring. Every morning when Favorito heard my voice his welcoming whinny would ripple out of the dark interior of the stalls. I'd bring him carrots, and walk him round and round in the ring until he was completely cooled down after we'd been out riding. If I let loose of his halter he would follow me around like a faithful dog until his knees would buckle and he'd drop into the thick dust for a roll on his back. But as though Pepe the Horse had an extra set of eyes mounted on the fence posts, he would invariably dash out yelling "*caballoooo*" in a threatening tone. He always put a stop to Favorito having a bit of pleasure as though getting dirty was such a terrible sin. After all, I could have just hosed off the dust. I don't know why I let Pepe set the rules for my beloved horse but I did, fearing that if we didn't both follow them, Favorito would pay for it later. Harsh was how it was at Pepe's stables.

From there we would ride out into the countryside that stretched into the hills. Some mornings we picked our way across the shallow river at the foot of the Phoenician Castle Sohail, and rode along the stretch of deserted beach west of town. The sunlight on the water made the sea shimmer like mercury. Between the whiteness of the horse and the whiteness of the sand and the dazzle off the water, everything became one blinding blaze of brilliance. Alone with this beautiful horse riding along the damp beach, his mane and my hair floating in the gentlest of sea breezes, was as close to heaven as I may ever know.

Other mornings, before the sun had risen hot in the sky, we'd cross the river higher up, where it was deeper, and follow a dusty road that wound up into the olive-tree-studded hills. I knew a place where a huge fig tree hung over the road and I'd urge Favorito forward with my knees until we were smack in the middle, its spicy fragrant leaves surrounding my face and his head. There I'd sit plucking off the *brevas,* the first crop of pale green figs of spring, their viscous white juice oozing from the branch. Favorito's canter was smooth and rhythmic, like rocking in a beautifully balanced chair, but often I was completely content for the two of us to amble along companionably, while I noticed the plump sheafs of green wheat ripening in the fields, or noted the vultures soaring in the morning thermals.

Castle Sohail

As we rode, I'd sing to him, a few lines in a minor key that like a whiff of fragrance is a time capsule. I sing it now and we are once again trotting along through the early morning dew. Those were the good times that don't keep me awake at night.

Then there were others. Times when I joined Pepe the Horse and one or more of the *señoritos*, the town's wealthy businessmen, and we trucked the horses into Málaga for the annual *feria*, that is as much elegant spectacle as anything, with beautiful horses and beautifully outfitted riders. As we rode proudly through the narrow streets waiters would rush out the doors of the local bars with tulip stemmed sherry glasses, handing them up filled with Tio Pepe or La Ina. The glasses were small enough but after three or four at different bars, my head would swim. Slick iron horseshoes on asphalt are a danger at the canter. You'd think that after Favorito fell the first time I would have learned. But I didn't. I was arrogant and besotted with our own reflection in the windows of yet another bar. And, as I squeezed my legs urging him into a canter, the stunning white horse slipped. Again. Heaven crashed heavily to earth. He could have broken one of his beautiful, slim legs or badly bruised his chest or ribs. Thank God, it was otherwise.

An English friend, Celia de Wolfe, who sometimes boarded her chestnut gelding at Pepe's stables, suggested we have our horses trucked to Sevilla so we could ride them in the famous spring *feria*. We must have made quite a handsome pair sitting tall and aristocratic in the saddle—raven-haired Celia on her handsome bronze horse, and blond me on Favorito. In the left hand we held the horse's reins lightly while the right hand was cocked with plenty of attitude at our hip. Just as a flamenco dancer, when you are dressed in *traje corto*—short jacket, ruffled white shirt, sombrero at a jaunty angle, fine leather boots—riding your handsome stallion, carriage and arrogance is all. One afternoon we were walking our horses side-by-side through the crowds of riders, aware of but not acknowledging admiring glances, when the American matador and painter, John Fulton, also riding a white stallion, rode over, introduced himself and praised Favorito's stunning good looks.

Lauren, Diana and Favorito in the feria

During those years I had terrible nightmares, almost always of a white stallion. Often he was about to be fatally gored in the bullring. In others he was carrying me away from scenes of vile death. In another he jumped a raging torrent to carry me safely away. It was always the same white stallion—Favorito. I would wake sobbing, shaken by what seemed so real, desperately grateful that it was only a bad dream. The nightmares of the white stallion don't come so often anymore. In the last one his huge dark eye locked on mine as his hooves clicked past on the damp concrete floor. And in the corner, draped supplely as an ermine coat tossed carelessly away, his hide was a pile of forlorn white. My dream horse had been skinned alive.

MAKING *LIMONADA*

No Room on the Ark

Ernest was an elephant, a great big fellow,
Leonard was a lion with a six foot tail,
George was a goat, and his beard was yellow,
And James was a very small snail.
— A.A. Milne, *The Four Friends*

When Frodo, our pig, was about a year and a half old his frantic squeals filtering up over the rooftops set off an alarm in our apartment one afternoon. I raced down to the pottery just as a little putt-putt van with an open back drove away with Frodo in the rear. I ran after the little truck but I couldn't catch it, and then in tears and near hysteria tore into the pottery to confront Pepe. "What have you done with Frodo?" I stormed at him. "Why didn't you tell me?" Anguished and furious with him, I was also furious with myself for not understanding what he and Carmela had planned from the beginning. The next time I saw Frodo he was stretched out on his back, eviscerated. A group of Spanish *señoras* was sitting around on low stools stuffing ground meat into long sausage casings that a short time before had been Frodo's intestines. I thoughtlessly blundered by bringing Lisa down to the pottery; with one glance my daughter nearly fainted in my arms. I grudgingly accepted some of the meat from Carmela but I didn't eat it, nor did Lisa. I don't think I completely trusted Pepe again after that betrayal.

In those years we had a parade of cats stroll through our lives. First, Phidippides, David's gray tabby, joined the zoo we called home. Fortunately by then we had moved to a big old dowager house on Calle José Antonio, *numero* 28. It's a good thing it was a cavernous house; we needed a barn just to house the animals. The floors were tiled, both upstairs and down. Glass doors at the back opened onto a commodious patio, with an old well in the center that years before had been filled in. Red and pink geraniums now cascaded down its sides. A small, dark stable was tucked in on the left side of the patio; it was a perfect place for our washing machine, except when the ground was damp I sometimes received an electrical shock. The bathroom, the only one for the house, sat in the far right-hand corner of the patio under the umber-leafed banana and castor trees. It was a tiny little room with what I called an elephant footbath, just large enough to sit, knees to chest. Hot water was heated instantly by a contraption that hung on the wall and fueled by butane from an orange *bombona* outside. Crossing the patio to the bathroom in the darkest hours of night—being careful to avoid stumbling over our sleeping Hurdy Gurdy, who no longer slept under his flowerpot—I'd look up and the sky would be an ocean of inky black with pinpoints of dazzling light. Sometimes I would stand, half-asleep, staring up, trying to memorize the essence of the old house and the enormity of the firmament, even then understanding that none of it would be mine forever.

David, who was eleven and highly analytical, once dropped Phidippides from the second floor window of his bedroom into the patio to see if she would land on her feet. "Mom, I wanted to see if cats really do have nine lives, and I guess she does," he explained in response to my protests. Then a mother cat and her three kittens, all tiny and pitifully thin, came into our lives. "You guys better find those kittens a home," Malcolm had warned in his characteristically humorous manner, but neither Lisa nor I took him seriously. By now he was losing patience and the threat was "find them homes or else." I'm sure we both promised but finding homes for kittens wasn't so easy. One day the tiny mother and her three black-and-white kittens disappeared. I knew from Malcolm's face that he'd done something but despite my pleading, begging and cajoling, he would never tell me what he'd done. My worst fear was that he had dropped them off out in the *campo* to fend for themselves and slowly starve to death. I was angry with him and with myself for not paying attention to his warning.

There must have been an invisible sign on the front of our door: all ye abandoned and discarded enter here. Soon, sensing that a spot had opened up, Amigito, a large, handsome white male cat, chose us. Amigito, who had the nasty habit of spraying when he came into the house, then lived in the street under our tiny white Seat 600 car, parked out front. His lovely white fur was always blackened with a stripe of axel grease down the center of his back. Other than the grease and his spraying, he was affectionate and devoted, if not to us then to our car.

The Franco years, despite the dark underbelly, were lovely times for children to grow up in a small Spanish town. They could come and go freely, playing with friends out on the street, often until quite late at night. David had two close friends: Jorge, who was Dutch, and Manolo, Spanish. The boys spent hours together doing the things boys do: riding bicycles, fishing, exploring. David and Marshall both spent much of their free time fishing from the breakwater down in the port of Fuengirola a few blocks away. They made their own fishing poles from the tall bamboo cane that grew out along the river that flowed down the red arroyos from the hills west of Mijas, the mountain town above Fuengirola. Before heading off to fish, they'd ride their bikes out to the river to catch frogs for bait. We laugh about the day I opened the tiny freezer of our old refrigerator and out jumped a bunch of small frogs. I suppose one or the other of my boys thought that they'd just stash their unused bait in the freezer. I don't know how long they were in there but frogs must have anti-freeze for blood because those little guys just hopped out and scared me thoroughly. I too hopped, straight up onto the red formica-topped kitchen table. My startled screeches amused my sons greatly.

That sign on our door attracted an elegant Gypsy horse-trader who would strut through town in his high-heeled boots and flat-brimmed, black Cordoban hat, a crisp hankie tucked in his jacket pocket. With his cane clicking the pavement in a rhythmic staccato he was the picture of an affected aristocratic English gentleman putting on airs. I bought what he assured me was a very pregnant miniature donkey and her little donkey cart. He patted her swollen belly to underscore the treat we had in store. What fun the children would have, I reasoned, riding through town in their little cart, pulled by what the Gypsy called an *enano*, a midget donkey.

That first Sunday we took the children, Hurdy Gurdy and Concha plus the tiny donkey and her cart for a picnic and swim out along the river. Hurdy Gurdy loved swimming in the river but even better was climbing onto my back where I lay floating on an air mattress. He also used his broad yellow beak to yank at the bottom of Lauren's little swimsuit. Who knew a duck could be part clown? Somehow we had managed to get out to the river but coming back the donkey couldn't or wouldn't pull the cart, so we tied Concha in front of the donkey with the little cart behind. The only creature that rode home in that tiny cart was Hurdy Gurdy. Thank goodness for brave little stouthearted Concha.

Lauren competing on Manolete

The donkey lived down in Arés's stable at Pepe's pottery. It soon enough became clear that the donkey wasn't pregnant, but I don't know whether she died of neglect and because I forgot to feed her, or if the pseudo-pregnancy was really some kind of growth that eventually did her in. I do know that Malcolm inherited the unpleasant task of hiring a crane and driver to rumble through town and hoist her tiny body over the rooftops and bury her out in the *campo*. To this day he relishes telling that story.

You'd have thought that by this time I would have known better, but it seems I had an unlimited capacity for making life difficult. I mean we weren't short of animals: We had Concha, Phidippides, Amigito, Favorito, Hurdy Gurdy. And now came serious trouble.

About this time I learned that Señor Giron, Francisco Franco's Minister of Education, who owned an enormous *finca*, an estate at the foot of the Phoenician castle at the western end of town, had a litter of Bull Mastiff puppies. (One of the few tidbits of Spanish gossip that leaked out in town was of the Phoenician artifacts that had been uncovered when the bulldozers dug the foundation in the sand for Minister Giron's estate. Rather than wait for archeologists to catalogue and remove the treasures, Giron ordered the bulldozers back to work.) Undaunted by archeological ruthlessness, I drove out to the Giron estate, introduced myself to Señora Giron, and asked for one of the puppies. We named her Nana and life was never again the same.

We awoke one morning to a chorus of woes:

"Mom, look at the toe of my shoe," hollered David.

"Mamá...*mis zapatos,*" wailed Lauren bursting into tears at the sight of her mangled sandals. Every pair of my children's shoes had chewed up toes, gnawed laces or holes chewed through the soles. We managed for a while, but unlike the Nana in Peter Pan, this Nana was more than I had bargained for. She was unruly and headstrong but in all fairness she was just an untrained puppy that needed time and training in order to fit into our large family.

One morning I came down and found that during the night Nana had killed Hurdy Gurdy. His lifeless little body was a mass of wet feathers dumped like a rag doll in the patio. From that moment I couldn't stand to look at Nana. Fortunately I knew an English lady, Daphne, who lived alone a long way out in the *campo*; I begged her to give Nana a home so I wouldn't have to see her again.

And for a while, even the thought of another creature joining our zoo was more than I could possibly bear. Until one afternoon some months later…

"Mom look," said Marshall, holding out a palm-sized green turtle. "I was coming home from fishing and down where the river empties into the sea was this little turtle walking along the sand. So I brought him home." The look of pride on his face at having rescued this little turtle was wonderful. Who was I to say "no"?

I had some raw hamburger in the refrigerator, so we put a little red enamel plate with small bits of meat outside the kitchen door. Marshall's turtle climbed hungrily into the plate and that's how we discovered that the turtle talked, making little growling sounds when he ate. So Marshall named him "Talking Turtle." Marshall built a small concrete pond under the clothes line and a ramp with slats on it, so that Talking Turtle could swim in his little pool underneath the sheets drying in the breeze. One summer, Malcolm's mother, Sylvia, the London grandma, was visiting, sleeping in Marshall's bedroom off the patio. One night she woke up and as she swung her feet down onto the tile floor, her toes curled around the shell of the sleeping turtle and provided her with quite a story to tell to her London friends. Another summer Marshall had a dozen tiny, newly hatched turtles crawling around the patio. One of us accidentally stepped on one, so Marshall scooped up all the babies, climbed on his bicycle and returned them to the river where he had found them.

Marshall's first yellow-headed parrot was a baby named Coco who very quickly learned to say his name.

"Coco," Marshall would coax him, and the baby parrot would echo "Coco." Marshall made the mistake of painting Coco's cage and Coco chewed the paint and got lead poisoning. He sat hunkered down on the floor of his cage, which I put next to my bed with a light bulb inside to raise the temperature and a blanket draped over the top to keep him warm. Thinking that he needed to drink, I tried to force him to take water, but he must have aspirated the drops and died within minutes in my hands. If only I had left well enough alone, but stupidly I thought I could help him. It was night and the house dark and silent but I woke up Marshall to tell him. I was so filled with remorse.

While I was out in the *campo* with my children one afternoon, I found what I was quite certain had to be the Guinness Book of World Records *thapo* or toad. He was an enormous, black warty old fellow I spied sitting along the riverbank. I took him home, weighed him and he came within a few ounces of the actual Guinness record holder toad. Fortunately we had a copy of the book on our bookshelf. I was so amazed and delighted by this creature that I carried him around the neighborhood to show him off to the neighbors. Curiously, no one seemed quite as awed or astonished as I was by the creature's size. Feeling a bit deflated, next day I drove him back out to the river and returned him to where he belonged.

There must be many families like ours who took in creatures with the best of intentions, yet have disaster stories to tell. Perhaps not quite as odd as the nocturnal hedgehog we took skiing to the Sierra Nevada, who slipped through a door left ajar to the balcony, fell into the snow and froze to death. Or the brain damaged kitten that used to screech pitifully, then topple over. Just thinking about all of it makes me feel weary and sad, but at the time I always thought that I could make a difference; hope always triumphed over reality.

MAKING *LIMONADA*

Perfidious

I was angry with my friend;
I told my wrath, my wrath did end.
I was angry with my foe;
I told it not, my wrath did grow.
— William Blake, A *Poison Tree*

Money pouring in from tourism was creating an epidemic of building and new businesses in Fuengirola and all along the coast. Old cottages were tumbling into rubble, and new construction, with a forest of long wooden poles supporting the upper floors, was erupting like weeds after spring rains. Pepe was not immune.

Out of necessity, and no doubt encouraged by Carmela, he began exploring ways to earn extra money. Their children were growing up and the responsibility of providing a good life for six of them, no matter how simply they lived and how inventive Carmela was, had to weigh heavily. His latest idea was to open a small shop where he would sell *cerámica*, both his own and decorative pieces he would purchase from the big pottery producers in Valencia. His oldest daughters, Isabel and MariCarmen, could work afternoons after school and Saturday mornings in the shop.

Pepe and María José

One day he asked if I would drive him in our van to make a quick tour of the Valencia potteries. Malcolm was agreeable as we would be gone just two days, and I assumed Carmela was as well. We would leave at dawn one morning, drive the whole day and be able to get to a few workshops in Valencia that afternoon. We'd visit a few more the following morning then drive back, arriving in Fuengirola late that second evening. It was tiring driving almost straight through for seven hours but Pepe was, as always, in good spirits and happy to tell me stories of his boyhood and make the kilometers and the hours go by more quickly.

"Pepito, ¿quiere pescado?" He began this story with the question he and the other village children used to ask Pepito, the mule that pulled the ice cart. "Pepito, want a fish? we'd ask. And Pepito would bob his head and we children would feed him a sardine or a hurele. Salvador, and his ice cart pulled by Pepito, walked all over town selling ice to the señoras and the fishermen. Sometimes Salvador would lift one or two of us up onto the wagon and we'd get to ride around the town. When I was a young boy," Pepe explained, "no one had refrigerators, so Salvador and Pepito were very popular. Salvador and my father were close friends who would go out together almost every night to Bar Tirita and sit at a table and talk with other friends and share bottles of wine. My father said that Salvador was a very intelligent man who knew a lot about politics and expressed his political ideas very clearly, but that he never advocated hurting anyone. All my father's friends liked their wine. They were never in a rush and ate and drank and talked until Bar Tirita closed.

On Sundays a group of seven or eight of them would take a dozen liters of wine out into the campo. A few would stay behind to prepare the fire and the makings for the paella and the rest of them would go off to hunt rabbits or birds. When the hunters returned they'd cook the paella over the fire and by the time they arrived back in town they had drunk all the wine."

"How did they get out into the *campo*?" I asked, since I couldn't imagine Spanish men trudging along with a big paella pan and all those liters of wine clutched in their arms.

"They rode in the ice cart pulled by Pepito. They took turns, a few riding and the rest walking, then they'd change places. They were never in a hurry," he said, throwing back his head and laughing. "My father always said what a good man Salvador was, but he was taken out late one night in 1938 and shot. I remember my father telling me that people, men and women too, just kept disappearing." Pepe's face became quite somber. "You were at risk if you talked politics or someone held a grudge against you and signed a *denuncia*," he reminded me. "Diana, have you heard about the man who was mayor of Mijas village before the war?"

"No, tell me." I shook my head, only briefly glancing at him in order to keep my eyes focused on the narrow road.

"His name is Manuel Cortes, and for thirty years he was hidden, first in a closet and then inside the walls of his house. His wife and daughter were the only ones who knew he was there and they never gave away his secret. The villagers suspected that Manuel might be hidden somewhere but although the *Guardía* searched for him and questioned his wife many times, they never found him. If the *Guardía* had discovered him before the amnesty, they would have thrown him into prison or executed him for being a Republican mayor and fighting for the Republic. "Can you imagine what it would be like to be in hiding in your own house for thirty years? Can you imagine keeping a secret in a small village when every *fulano* knows every *fulana's* affairs? Not to be able to walk about the town, not to be out in the fresh air? I can't imagine living like that for thirty years," he admitted. "But I guess he didn't have much choice."

"Tell me about the amnesty," I asked when we had stopped for a mid-morning coffee at a bar along the road. He was lighting a cigarette but he shook his head and nodded almost imperceptibly in the direction of the car. I understood his reticence immediately and changed the subject to the type of ceramics he was thinking of buying in Valencia.

When we were back on the road, I once again asked Pepe to tell me about the amnesty. "I think it was the year you first came to the pottery, in 1969. To celebrate the thirtieth anniversary of their victory in the Civil War, Franco's government declared an amnesty for all crimes committed during the war, including the crime of having fought for the other side, for the Republic. And a few days later, Manuel Cortes came out of hiding. He'd been a socialist mayor, and by most accounts a very good and fair one. But few socialists survived the war or the repression and retaliation that came after. I've heard rumors that during or just after Málaga fell, the Franco rebels hanged the mayor of Fuengirola, although my father never talked to me about it. The mayors of Alhaurin, Benalmadena and Los Boliches were all shot or died in prison, but I don't know any more about them than that…" He stopped talking as though to let the somber history speak for itself.

I was mostly unimpressed with the Valencia pottery workshops. Everything seemed mass produced using molds instead of hand throwing on a wheel. The work was decorated by hand but the designs were pretty unimaginative and once you'd seen a few pieces of each design they all started losing their individuality. But Pepe was pretty sure he could sell this work so he placed orders at three of the factories we visited. Although I had understood that he needed the van to bring back some of what he bought, it turned out that he had to place orders that would be shipped directly to his new shop.

Meanwhile, back in Fuengirola, Malcolm had taken the kids out for ice cream that evening and they were walking along the Pasco Maritimo when he saw Carmela walking with her children. She took one look and realized who it was that had driven her husband to Valencia. Pepe had apparently not told her and I can only imagine her shock and anger.

On our return I was tired from so much driving and rested up for another day or two. Leaving the pottery one afternoon a few days later, I met Carmela as she was walking in through the narrow passageway. The look on her face was one of cold fury. "Diana, I trusted you as a friend." That was all she said. It would be many years before I ever set foot in the pottery again.

Pepe the Horse

*Cante jondo...is the trilling of birds, the song
of the rooster, and the music of the forest and
fountain...the duende climbs up inside you, from
the soles of the feet.*

— Federico García Lorca

The wealthy ranchers—the *señoritos* of the town—
called the little stable man "Pepino." (Diminutives
are big in Andalucía.) Our family called him Pepe
the Horse because in the town of Fuengirola, as my Godson,
José, once laughingly pointed out years later, almost every
man was called Pepe, Paco or Manolo. If you didn't know
someone's name you were always safe with one of those
three, José advised me. He was right. It could get confusing.

What was certain was that Pepe the Horse, a small runt
of a fellow, had an inferiority complex and trouble holding his liquor. Yet he carried his slender frame with the
haughty, ramrod straight back of a Parisian model. Despite
his natural dignity he carelessly tossed it all away when he
was drunk. He was also fond of the most expensive Cuban
cigars—a Monte Cristo, the brand smoked exclusively by the

señoritos—and when he wasn't smoking one—the end all mangled and soggy—his thin lips were glued to a cigarette. He always wore a clean starched shirt tucked into his dark gray, calf length riding pants. I think he may have even slept in his supple Spanish riding boots with their line of hand stitching down the sides and around the gently pointed toes. He had his boots handmade in Sevilla with a slightly canted heel that gave his small frame several needed inches.

Hats were important to Pepe the Horse. Heading home to his mother's for lunch, his battered turquoise motorbike hiccuping noisily as it struggled for traction in the deep dust, he had a black and white checkered cap pulled down on his forehead. Mounted on the back of a beautiful Spanish stallion, he wore a *sombrero* Cordobés, the flat-brimmed riding hat of Andalucía. Vanity was clearly Pepe's middle name, and with so little hair, a hat was essential to his sense of style. Once in a while I caught a glimpse of his pale scalp and the wisps of long hair that he'd plastered in a sweep to hide his baldness. He didn't have much money either so when he wasn't sleeping at the stable he lived with his mother, but the small man had huge pride and an even bigger sense of style. Pride, style and dignity. And generosity. He had the gracious generosity inborn in every Spaniard of his generation, regardless of their status.

There wasn't a stallion in Pepe's stable that wasn't a knockout beauty. Andalucian horses are known not only for their thick necks, beautiful heads and elegant conformation but also for their gentle, noble nature and their willing hearts. So it was always a mystery to me why the bits were so punishing and the steel nosepieces had sharp pointed teeth. I guess I explained away the insensitivity I saw by rationalizing that you can't have suffered as the Spaniards suffered during and after their Civil War and still have compassion for animals. Besides, it was a strictly hierarchical society, and the lowly four-legged creatures were at the bottom, lower even than the Gypsies.

Apart from Favorito, the horses in Pepe's care were owned by the wealthy ranchers who rode them—oftentimes a bit unsteadily—on Sundays and holidays, when they would ride out in the company of their men friends to their *cortijos,* their ranches in the countryside. Otherwise, the horses were parked, like so many fine Italian racing cars, in the stable that Pepe ran up beyond the bullring.

From our house I would walk each morning straight up Calle José Antonio, cross the *carretera,* and head up past the *plaza de toros* and the *parque zoológico* to the big riding ring outside the stables. Pepe was often out in the ring putting one of his beautiful charges through their paces. The man and the horse were a study of beauty in motion; I never tired of watching or trying to detect some secret and subtle movement on Pepe's part that communicated silently to that elegant mass of rippling muscle and flowing mane. Round and round at the canter, forward, back, sidestepping, horse's head erect, gorgeous thick neck arched until its mouth was flecked with foam and its sides heaving and wet from exertion. Even when Pepe rode Favorito, I could never detect nor replicate his exact hand and leg movements so I could never get my beloved horse to dance with me with the same grace as he did with Pepe. I was an excellent rider and spent hours every day practicing in the ring, often riding bareback to strengthen and deepen my seat, working diligently to perfect the dressage routines. But I've often wondered if Pepe didn't deliberately hold back explaining crucial techniques so he didn't have a woman and an *extranjera* at that, being as glorious with her horse as he was.

Pepe always called me "Doña Diana" as though I was of a higher status than he. As much as I fancied myself quite Spanish in temperament, my egalitarian views from California were just part of who I was. So it was natural for me to befriend Pepe and that perhaps was part of the problem.

Despite his courtesy to all the horses' owners, Pepe the Horse had a cruel streak. He was tough on those horses and when a hissed"*caballo*" rolled out of his mouth, those horses knew to move aside, stand still and behave or else. Many times I saw Pepe bring back a horse with the bridge of its nose bloodied raw by the steel-toothed nosepiece that bit savagely into bone. I frequently saw ruby rakes along a horse's sides where Pepe's spurs had cut deeply after some infraction or another. The horses and their care were his life, his passion, and his profession. He gave them shots, cleaned and groomed them, trained them. But like a harsh, demanding parent he brooked no misbehavior. His word was law and he demanded split-second obedience. In the hierarchy of Andalucía only in the stable was the little man king.

From the beginning I understood that Pepe was a lonely man, hungry for friendship and acceptance, so the day he invited me to ride out and have lunch with him at a *venta* on the old *carretera* to Coín, I said yes. He was quite excited to introduce me to what he described as a "*plato sabroso*," a delicacy of the season. I can only guess at my expression when the cook carried out a red clay *cazuela* still bubbling with hot olive oil, filled with large chunks of garlic, tiny songbirds with their little feathered heads still attached and a small black fly. I didn't have the heart or the courage to refuse to eat them, avoiding the fly of course, but after a few icy *copitas* of Tio

Pepe it bothered me less. However, a tiny sliver of light had illuminated the cultural divide I was trying to ignore. It was during such a lunch that I tried to point out that the *señoritos* were just men like himself, but they had the good fortune to have come from families with land and money. That was the only difference between them. He politely nodded his agreement, as though he understood, but he couldn't really, because he had been a product of the patriarchal system of Andalucía since the day he was born. His response was to call out "*¡otra copita! hombre*," and order another drink.

Pepe would occasionally drop by our house at Calle José Antonio 28. The hammering of the doorknocker would reverberate through the tile-floored, high-ceilinged rooms. After Pepe shook hands with every member of our family and bowed courteously and tipped his hat to my daughters and me, he'd hastily replace his hat back on his bald head. He'd park his cigar with its wet mangled end on the edge of a bookcase or a table. Then he'd rock back on the rear legs of one of the wicker-caned chairs, close his eyes as if in a trance, and out of his throat would float one of the minor key Flamenco melodies with all the pain and anguish and Adam's apple throbbing intensity that the songs and their words required. These a capella bursts accompanied by crisp handclaps to accentuate the beat, were mesmerizing but also a bit funny, although we tried hard to maintain straight faces to avoid hurting his feelings. The themes of his songs were of betrayal and anguish, wild-eyed horses, and the life and loves of gypsies. Did Pepe, an unlettered man, know the roots of the music he sang, of the tragic expulsion of the Moors, Jews and Gypsies centuries before? Of the brutality, persecution and inferiority…the wail of the grieving soul that the music expressed? Consciously, perhaps not. But the marrow of his bones was knowing. When Pepe closed his eyes and what García Lorca called "the stammering suffering" of his voice rose up, he just slipped away from the world. It didn't matter what we were doing. Suddenly we had a flamenco concert in our house.

After a few songs he'd tell stories of times he had ridden a particularly high-spirited horse in the bullring. He would rise from the chair and plant his boots firmly in the dust of the ring (our tiled floors), all four feet nine inches of his body pulled tall, rigidly arching his back with his pelvis thrust forward to taunt the bull and death. He would tuck in his chin and his arms would float up as he called to the bull from his nervously dancing horse, "*toro je je.*" And in one graceful arc, he'd lean in close and thrust the imaginary *banderillas* into the back of the charging bull, and at the last instant, curve his horse away from the razor sharp horns. His cigar butts or cigarette ashes would be ground under the stacked heel of his riding boots. He was so caught up in the drama of his bullfight or his flamenco that he literally forgot where he was. It was always quite a performance. But imaginary. The chance in the bullring that he never had.

More than once I saw Pepe the Horse get a bit sloppy and unpleasantly amorous when he had drunk too much Tio Pepe. Despite his rough edges and severity with the horses, and despite having to shove him away from time to time, there was still something very likeable about the little man. Maybe it was because I could always feel how desperately hard he tried to be accepted by the town's *señoritos*, men of inherited means, whose lives revolved around wine, women and a good time, with the wealth to support their habits.

Sure they would invite him for a few drinks for entertainment value if he happened to come into a bar where they were gathered.

"Pepino, *!Una copita! hombre*" they would sing out from their own Tio Pepe haze of bonhomie—but he was never accepted as anything other than a *cateto*, a lowly stable man who happened to be highly skilled with horses. And a poor, sloppy drunk at best.

Pepe the Horse wore his clothes not with the careless ease of one of the town's *señoritos*, but with the studied care and attention to detail of a man without status and means, a bit like the *hidalgos* of Cervantes' time: *Hidalgos* were men so poor they hadn't anything to eat, yet would lounge conspicuously against the door frames of their houses with a toothpick in their teeth, so that the passing world would think them to have just relished a fine meal. It was that glimpse of his humanity and vulnerability that has made Pepe indelible.

MAKING *LIMONADA*

La Romería del Rocío

As the day ends, the birds in the Cork Oak Tree
at the edge of the marsh fall quiet. It is as if the
huge red bell of the sun—pealing for silence—
had rung the Angelus.
— Juan Antonio Fernández, *Doñana: Spain's Wildlife Wilderness*

F ive sherry besotted princes of Andalucía and one thirty-year-old California Jewish blond, six days on horseback sleeping out at night in tents, a fervent religious procession in which thousands lose their senses honoring an ancient statue of a virgin—what a recipe for delirium!

It was spring, 1972, and I was still practically the only young woman in Fuengirola who rode horses. Of course it helped that I owned a beauty. Many of the local ranchers kept elegant, thick-necked stallions at Pepe's stables, but they only rode during the annual feria and on the occasional weekends.

Alvaro Domecq, the famed *rejoneador* and son of the Domecq sherry family from Jerez de la Frontera along the Atlantic coast—the region fabled for their fine wines, their beautiful daughters and their stunning horses—invited a few of these ranchers to join him and his *hermandad*, his brotherhood of celebrants, on a religious pilgrimage, La Romería del Rocío. And they invited me.

Age and a bit of wisdom have allowed me to see that I was purely a novelty, invited along for their amusement. But I didn't know that then. My Spanish was good, not great, which was just fine since any rough spots in the conversation went right over my head. This allowed the men to relax and have fun. I didn't know exactly what to expect but was nothing if not game for an adventure. So I proposed to the English language magazine *Lookout* that I would write a feature story on this historic Romería del Rocío. I read James Michener's *Iberia*, and learned that this pilgrimage, held every year on the seventh Sunday following Easter, dates back to the thirteenth-century after the Moors had been expelled from Granada. As the legend goes, a homely little wooden statue of the Virgin was discovered in a tree trunk by a hunter from the village of Almonte, in the province of Huelva, where she had probably been hidden to protect her from desecration by the Moorish infidels. Over the following centuries a cult-like following has built up in her honor.

That sounded intriguing, so I pulled together the required formal riding attire, piece by piece. First a black, flat brimmed, sombrero Cordobes that someone lent me. (As I look at a 1972 copy of *Lookout* magazine, my face on the cover looks like I am wearing a pimple on my head. The hat is way too small. But I didn't understand these fine distinctions at the time.) I bought a pair of leather chaps called *zahones* that cover the rider's legs, only my pair was a few inches too short and didn't drape nicely down to my boots. But I didn't know that either. I had just two—for six dusty days—of the white, lace-fronted shirts that all the men and the few women who rode Amazona wore. (Amazona refers to the women who ride astride their horses, dressed in classic riding attire—*traje corto*—as I would dress, as opposed to the women who ride sidesaddle in long, gaily-colored Flamenco dresses.) We would be camping out for the week, so someone lent me a small tent.

Lookout Magazine   Mike Lewin photo

On the morning we left, Malcolm, his face mottled-gray with early morning stubble, leaned against the doorframe of our old whitewashed house. He wore a tattered terry cloth bathrobe the color of the Mediterranean that lapped a few blocks from our door. He stood on one bare leg, one foot at an awkward angle on top of the other, minimizing his exposure to the cold marble doorstep. An expression of curiosity and pride were overlaid in his eyes with a tinge of sadness and envy that he couldn't quite hide. He wasn't invited. Yet ever the good sport, he managed a regal Queen Elizabeth wave of his hand, wishing us all well, as the faded green Land Rover pulled away heading south. How I wished that he hadn't been standing there in his bare feet and bathrobe for all the men to see. It made it look like I was heading off on a lark with all these Spanish men, leaving my husband and four young children behind. Of course that's exactly what I was doing, but I tried not to see it. I'd been offered a chance at what promised to be a wonderful experience and my personal philosophy has always been to say yes to life.

So there I was, blond hair pulled back, covering a fake "fall," a hairpiece that allowed blond hair to cascade down my back. (The quintessential photograph of a beautiful woman riding a handsome white horse in the spring Feria of Sevilla, is taken from the rear, and shows her blond hair pulled back, tied with a black ribbon, streaming down her back.) I had the glorious white horse. I had the invitation. What I lacked was long enough hair. So my horseback riding hairdresser, Rosendo, who understood the importance of these things, got to work. The fall was so firmly attached to the back of my head with hairpins that my head felt trussed in a corset. Rosendo had sworn that no amount of cantering or trotting would shake it loose.

These men were pals, jokers and storytellers all, with big personalities; the spirit of that drive was one of laughter rico-cheting about. They talked so fast that I wasn't always sure I got the joke or the entire story, but I laughed anyway. When the effort became too intense I studied the landscape, softly verdant and rolling, the nearer to the Atlantic we drove.

I heard a few growling stomachs, including my own, by the time we arrived in Sanlúcar de Barrameda, at the mouth of the Guadalquivir River, southwest of Sevilla. The eight of us piled into a modest restaurant looking out at the river we were soon to cross. We virtually inhaled fried anchovies, called *boquerones*, from the local waters, piling their heads, tiny tails and bones back on the white plates. Using chunks of heavy country bread we scooped up *ensaladilla rusa*—potato salad with shrimp and lemony mayonnaise. Our waiter brought platter after platter: salad greens drenched with dark olive oil, scattered with tuna and grated carrot for color—I loved the way the men dove in communally with their forks spearing pieces of lettuce and tomatoes and green *manzanilla* olives. I ate my share of crisp fried calamari rings drenched in lemon juice, and the mounds of tiny amber fish called *chanquetes*, which we scooped up with our fingers and dropped into our open mouths, heads, tails and all. They're so tiny that all you get is a delicious crunch of flavor. (Years later, when fishermen started coming back with empty boats, Spain discovered that these tiny treasures, devoured by the ton, were really the infant fish—the *cria*—of all the major species.) *Gambas al ajillo*—plump rosy prawns—emerged from the kitchen in red clay *cazuelas*, still sizzling in a torrid bath of golden olive oil and garlic. As if still alive, these sweet juicy morsels jumped out of their baths and into our mouths, then we sopped up the oil with crusts of bread. And we drank the local wine and plenty of it. These men were Spaniards and Andalucians, and eating and drinking heartily is part of the joy of living. I had no difficulty matching them in spirit. Any thoughts of home faded away.

Centuries earlier, just before they set sail for the New World in their caravels, the crews of Columbus and Magellan had made this same pilgrimage to El Rocío that we were to embark on. Sanlúcar sits with choppy gray foam of the Atlantic on one side, while inland, vineyards roll across the landscape. This tiny region produces *manzanilla*, the wine that would dampen our parched, and dust-dried throats for the next week. It's as pale as early morning sunlight and the locals told me that I might be able to taste a hint of the Atlantic Ocean in its delicate flavor. I don't recall drinking even one glass of water during the entire week.

On the beach in front of us, our three men Friday, who would serve us as butlers, stable hands and drivers, had assembled our horses. They had been trucked down, nose to tail, in a big open-topped van. I was reassured to see that my beloved Favorito had made the trip safely. They were a handsome lot—dappled grays, chestnuts, and Favorito, dazzling white. They were about to be re-loaded onto a ferry for the crossing to the other side of the river where we would begin our long ride. I watched the bucking ferry's wooden ramp flapping about in the waves, but the Andalucian horse is so noble that they made little fuss and clattered up the ramp. They must have been glad to be out of that van and eager to feel the wind in their ears.

We were a motley lot: playboy ranchers, Luís, Matias, and Cristobal, Pepe Casada, whose father raised fighting bulls in the province of Cadiz, Felipe, a waiter in Fuengirola's Bar Casino who had been graced with an especially generous gift of wit and a wicked tongue, an English photographer, Mike Lewin, who had lived in Spain so long that he thought in Spanish, and me. Also along were two old Land Rovers loaded with our tents, sleeping bags, cases of wine, and the three drivers. A stately white ram with big curving horns was tied to the back of one of the vehicles and trudged his way along breathing dust and exhaust. A few days later this fine fellow would become grilled lamb chops for a host of guests who visited our camp on horseback. We crossed the mouth of the Guadalquivir River where it empties into the Atlantic Ocean on the wheezy old flat-bottomed ferry, the crazily overloaded Land Rovers rocking and swaying in the swells. The ferryman, in his rolled-up pants and bare feet, warbled songs of El Rocío into the wind while he clapped out acapella rhythms with his calloused palms.

The following morning we joined with brotherhoods of riders and gaily bedecked wagons from Sanlúcar and Jerez de la Frontera who were awaiting the arrival of Princess Doña Sofía, the wife of Prince Juan Carlos, Franco's chosen heir to the Spanish throne. While we waited, plates of olives, manchego cheese, bread and chorizo appeared mysteriously from the wagons. Suddenly, like a bright cloud, the princess and her attendants arrived riding sidesaddle, their gaily-colored flamenco dresses rippling down their horses' flanks. At last our cavalcade was on its way, led by our host, Alvaro Domecq, carrying the flag of his province of Jerez de la Frontera.

Our path lay through the largest game reserve in Western Europe: Las Marismas—the marshes—of the Coto de Doñana, owned by the World Wildlife Fund. The Coto had once been the private hunting reserve of Spanish sovereigns, visited by famous bullfighters, European royalty and artists like Francisco Goya. We saw, as they must have seen, herds of red deer, wild boar with bristly hides and curving bone-white tusks, and thousands of birds: cattle egrets with yellow feet and beaks and black and white storks with persimmon-colored bills and long hinged legs. From time to time I could catch sight of an Imperial eagle soaring far overhead. For long hours we rode, often Favorito and I alone, without another rider in sight, through dense Italian Stone pine forests. The cones and needles of these trees had been carpeting these untrodden paths for centuries and the trail was soft and springy under Favorito's hooves, aromatic with the scent of resin and the sea. In places all that remained were craggy carcasses of pines that had been smothered by sand. Another sentinel of the Coto de Doñana is the cork oak, wrapped in its thick blanket of spongy bark. Quite suddenly the conifers faded, the oaks disappeared and we were riding through a desert of lonely, undulating sand dunes, stretching on to the Atlantic Ocean due west. I had been warned to be alert for quicksand but had no idea what to look for so I placed my trust completely in my horse.

Our journey was frequently broken by stops for dance and song, plates of cheese, bread and chorizo, and lots and lots of wine. On one break, while Mike, the photographer and I were making an exploratory round of the hospitality, we were suddenly yanked off our feet, our hats whisked off and we were officially baptized with a bottle of *manzanilla* poured over our heads becoming genuine Rocieros. Mike's Nikon camera got a good dousing which jammed the shutter, but no one took this seriously, most of all Mike. It was as though a joyous sense of carefree exhilaration had enveloped us all, and this giddy lightheartedness was to continue for the full trip. At the end of the trek we worked out that each member of our group divided by the bottles of wine drunk divided by the number of days equaled five bottles per person per day. It was clearly no time to think of my liver.

During those long hours swaying in the saddle, I composed a song to Favorito, and sang it to him over and over:

"Favorito, *caballo bonito*,
¿*Cómo estás mi* Favorito?"

Though we were both very weary I like to think the minor key melody and my voice were soothing to him.

Toward midnight, through heavy eyes, I finally glimpsed the flickering lights of the sixteenth-century royal Palace of Doñana, our camp for the second night. (Years later I would do research on Doñana and discover that many historians believe that Francisco Goya painted his lover, the Duchess of Alba, there during the time she owned the vast estate.) That night, however, speculative art history was the last thing on my mind. With the smell of wood fires and hot food floating in the still night air, I fell into my sleeping bag—I can't remember feeling such complete exhaustion in my life—with just enough strength left to pull off my boots.

One of Mike's photographs, taken the following morning, shows Luís and Cristobal, their faces covered with lather, using the mirror of the Land Rover to guide the strokes of their razors. Another photo shows Favorito covered with a plaid blanket, so I must have remembered to attend to him before I succumbed to sleep.

We soon swung into our saddles and began riding through vast areas of lush fern and lavender, miles perfumed by rosemary and wildflowers and endless groves of eucalyptus. Towards late afternoon we could see in the distance the town of El Rocío and a great cloud of dust hanging over it. We rode in tired and dusty but full of excitement at the sight of hundreds of great ox carts and the thousands of riders and their beautiful companions attired in multicolored flamenco dresses. We had ridden back in time, into an earlier century.

Imagine throngs of jubilant pilgrims, hundreds of gypsy families and their caravans, a haze of ever-present red dust kicked up by the hooves of horses, their riders wearing the flat crowned, wide-brimmed Cordoban felt hats with a grosgrain black ribbon worn on the jut of the chin as an anchor. Hand-made leather *zahones* decorated with intricate white catgut covered the riders' legs down to the wide, iron stirrups. (Look at any painting of Spanish nobility in the Prado Museum. You will see the same lethal-looking iron stirrups.) Beautiful women rode sidesaddle, their sleek dresses had bold flounces at elbow and ankle, and intricately fringed scarves draped about their long golden necks. Vivid colors sang out of the gaiety and celebratory essence of life. Stout oxen with jubilantly adorned headdresses pulled tall covered carts festooned with white and red pom-poms. I could catch glimpses within of dark eyes and wide smiles of the children and the grandmothers wrapped in black shawls. Sound was a constant: the soft low of the oxen, the rhythmic strum of guitars and big wooden drums, the high pitched voices of reed flutes and wooden recorders and the sharp staccato of handclaps. Try to envision days and nights of ever flowing wine, dancing and no sleep, all in heady tribute to a small, beloved wooden statue of a Virgin with many names—Our Lady of the Dew, Nuestra Señora del Rocío, La Blanca Paloma, the White Dove. That's the Romería del Rocío.

We joined the colorful parade of horses and riders that wound slowly through the village, then passed in front of the basilica to offer our homage to the Virgin. We rode three abreast so that I was flanked on either side by one of my elegant but dusty companions. (We were told many times that week that ours were the finest horses there. I learned later that everyone leaves their best horses at home because the journey is grueling. While we, being eager first-timers, had ridden our best.) This parade continued through the night, with flares and fireworks illuminating the darkness. Festive faces lit in the phosphorescence added an air of carnival madness straight out of a Goya etching.

Monday the Virgin is carried through the streets on her silver throne. Only the men from the town of Almonte are allowed to carry her and any outsider who tries to muscle his way in is hastily dealt with, sometimes rather brutally with a chop on the head or shoulders. Mike told me of rolling one such unfortunate off to the side so he wouldn't be trampled under the feet of the 250,000 pilgrims.

The tiny Virgin rocked, she teetered precariously, she was almost alive; I was certain she would topple into the dust in the turmoil. But faithful hands always steadied her. The crowd was so dense that she moved only a few yards at a time. Outstretched hands pressed flowers on her throne, people scrambled to touch her hem. And overhead, little children tumbled from arm to outstretched arm so they could kiss her. I saw one small child, not more than two or three years old, somersaulting through the air from one pair of up-stretched hands to the next.

Except for the solemn pandemonium of the procession with the Virgin, all was merrymaking and song. Even in the basilica, the ceremony was broken with lusty shouts

"¡Viva La Blanca Paloma! Long live the White Dove." "¡Viva!" the crowd bellows back. "¡Viva la Virgen del Rocío! Long live the Virgen of El Rocío." "¡Viva!" a thousand voices answer.

"¡Viva la Reina de Las Marismas! Long live the Queen of the Marshes." "¡Viva!" they shout joyously, their voices growing hoarse and cracking with strain.

Many communities in southern Spain own a house in this village of El Rocío, occupied only this one week of the year. At each of these houses the people held their local priest aloft. And he, with arms outstretched, chanted his praises to the Virgin, shouting to be heard above the din. We were greeted as cherished friends and urged to drink and eat, while the singing and dancing continued on through the night.

Ah the spontaneous dancing...I loved to dance the Sevillanas...they are gay and light in spirit with elegant out-stretched arms, twirling hands that curve and call, flashing eyes, artfully arching backs...the footwork is intricate and the patterns for each short set are different yet variations on the theme. (I danced almost every dance but never quite got the sequence of the sets. I frequently seemed to zig when I should have been zagging. But nobody seemed to mind or even notice.) Voices called out encouragement to the danc-ers... "¡Qué güasa tiene la niña! What spirit the girl has!" Enthusiastic palms cracked out the complex rhythms...the ruffled hems of dresses twirled away and swung back in rip-ples of color, boots stamped the dust with a provocative air of insouciance. Sevillanas are like the first sweet teasing play of boys and girls exploring their delicious differences.

All around me, always were songs of the Rocío:"El embarque de ganou...levanta una polvorea...sung in the relaxed, last vowel swallowing díalect of Andalucía.

The days and nights passed in a blur of wine, dancing and horses, yet all too soon it was time to begin the long, dusty trek home. Soon we were back at the Guadalquivir River with an invitation to continue the revelry that night in the winery of Perez Meggia. And what a last night celebration it was: sampling the varieties of wines of the bodega—extracted with a long glass tube right out of the wooden barrels—and dancing Sevillanas among the fragrant casks.

Dancing the Sevillanas   Mike Lewin photo

At home once again I sat at my typewriter, the house mostly silent except for the faint whispered exhalations of my husband and children sleeping in the drafty old rooms, and struggled to capture in words an experience so elusive. I had a feeling of having awakened from a delirious dream, a delicious trance that had enveloped me. On my lips remained a faintly salty tang of fragrant breezes through *las marismas*; the sounds of music, dance and laughter still vibrated in my ears. I was, for a brief moment only, part of a beautiful archaic world of innocence and ritual, which invaded my eyes and imagination, pure as primary color.

Whenever I sip a glass of *manzanilla*, it's not just an elixir of the Atlantic I search for, but for a memory of the magic seduction of that time and the curious legend of La Romería del Rocío.

A *Finca* in Coín

Soul of fibre and heart of oak.
— Cervantes, *Don Quijote*

Over the rutted and dusty-red back roads from Fuengirola, a bicycle ride to the village of Coín took about two hours, one my younger son Marshall often made to visit his friends, Paco and his wife Paca, and their young son, Francisco.

Our family first met Paco and Paca when we drove out to visit our Fuengirola neighbors, Patzi and John Gordon Davis. John had bought an old farmhouse, a country place on a plateau of small *fincas* called Los Llanos that overlooked Coín below. Here John would be able to write his novels in the peaceful quiet of the countryside, away from the racket of motorbikes and noisy street life of town.

Paco and Paca's *finca* adjoined John's, so the two men agreed that Paco would work and plant John's rich loamy soil in addition to his own land. Clear water bubbled generously from a nearby spring and fed the *acequia*, a narrow canal that irrigated the tomatoes, onions and garlic that Paco grew with such success. The spring was so abundant that it created a languidly flowing river that ambled past the foot of both *fincas*. The fragrance of the earth mingled with the fecund banks of the river made the soft breezes that swept over the farmland as sweet as the friendship that grew between Marshall and his new friends.

Paca and Paco

Their *finca* wasn't a grand place, just a few acres and two whitewashed rooms. The rooms were separated by an open-air caned roof covered with grapes hanging down in heavy bunches. That patio is where the family lived during the warm months, and being inland in Andalucía, that meant most of the year.

In one room Paco stored feed for the pigs—Paca was almost always raising a white sow and her small piglets in a little alcove tucked under the roof that sloped down to the river. Along with feed for the pigs, Paco also stored grain for the chickens and laid out the harvested onions and garlic to dry and put the crates of tomatoes that he and his brother, Antonio, harvested from the rows of robust green plants that grew shoulder high. If you walked between those rows of tomatoes and brushed against the foliage, the spicy sweet scent would layer like perfume on your skin. Paco could grow red onions half the size of a basketball, so fertile was this farmland.

Underneath the bunches of hanging grapes was a sturdy table covered in cheery red oilcloth. That was the table where they sat to eat their meals, and where Paca chopped garlic, onions and tomatoes for her Sunday *arroz*.

Paca's kitchen was just a corner between two stuccoed walls with an opening where she built the fire. Soot covered the walls around the fireplace, yet every spring and summer she whitewashed the tiny space despite knowing that the flames would always make short order of the pristine white. To the right of the open fireplace was a small gas stove fueled by a large orange canister—*una bombona*—of gas. Out of that tiny kitchen Paca produced delicious *arroz*—not Carmela's paella to be sure, but delicious nonetheless. Every Sunday and often during the week as well, Paca made her *arroz*. Considering that she had to hand carry everything to the *finca* from the village—they didn't own a car—Paca's food was homey, filling and comforting. Most importantly it was made with love and served with a radiant smile.

In the other room, directly opposite the storeroom, was a mattress and pillows that they shared with their young son, Francisco, their only child, named after his father. (Names in Coín were as potentially confusing as anywhere in Spain at the time. Paca's real name was Josefa and Paco's was Francisco yet everyone called him Paco. And Marshall's real name was Marshall but their family called him "Juan.") Paca told me that one day, early in their friendship, "Juan" asked her: "*¿Te importa si te llamo* Paca? Would you mind if I call you Paca?" And Paca she has been ever since. In this windowless dark room Paca also kept the coffee pot, the eating utensils and the room temperature amber bottles of San Miguel beer that Paco was quick to offer a guest.

"*Niña, traele un cervecita a* Diana," he would call out to her from his spot on a cane thatched stool under the grapevines where he sat resting after long hours in the fields. And Paca, wrapped in her old checkered apron, would come out of her tiny kitchen to fetch the beer from the storeroom. Presently she'd place a dish of green *manzanilla* olives, slices of chorizo and rough country bread on the table, simple *tapas* to keep the beer company. One does not drink without eating any-where in Spain.

Marshall and Francisco were buddies despite about five years difference in their ages. Francisco loved it when Marshall bicycled out to spend the weekend or came during summer vacation to work in the fields with Paco. The boys almost looked like brothers; each one had large expressive eyes, dark hair and they shared the same sweet disposition.

I would drive out to the *finca* over the same bumpy roads, about an hour in our small Seat 600, and somehow, no matter how long it had been since I last visited, Paca would see me coming and be out in the rutted lane wearing her apron, waving her arms hello. They were always happy to see me, their beaming grins left no doubt. I was utterly content walking with Paca down to her rows of robust green butter lettuce. With her kitchen knife she would cut off a large glis-tening head, and continue on down to the *acequia*, where the clear water flowed at a steady pace; she'd swish the head about, then wrap it in a clean dish towel and carry it back to her little lean-to of a kitchen with me trotting at her heels. Her salad preparation was simple and involved sprinkling the leaves with course sea salt and drizzling them with dark olive oil. Never have I tasted a salad that could compare with Paca's. No onion, no tomatoes, just the glorious fresh greens, olive oil and salt. That salad epitomized what I loved about Paco and Paca: simple, earthy and honest.

We were sitting in the cool shade under the grape arbor one Sunday, having a San Miguel beer and talking while Paca cooked *arroz*. I asked Paco how he and Paca had met. "We lived in Coín," he told me, lifting his battered straw hat off his head and mopping his forehead with a kerchief, "and *la niña* was from Mijas." Paco always called his wife "*niña*." "She came to work to help my mother; she was just a young girl of ten or twelve and my mother liked her because she was a hard worker. So she stayed working for us...nobody had any money in those days after the *Guerra Civil*, but my mother gave her a place to sleep and her food and that helped her family in Mijas since they had one less mouth to feed. And after a few years my mother told me that *la niña* should become my *novia*. And that's how it happened," he said, throwing back his head and laughing at the memory. Like all Andalucians, Paco was always laughing and always telling stories, but his Andalucian dialect was so strong, that I often had a bit of trouble following what he was telling me, so I said "*si, si*" a lot. ("*Claro*," clearly, also never let me down, since it worked well for just about any conversation and was almost always an appropriate response.) But this story I understood.

"Paco, don't you remember how your mother wanted you to be *novios* with a rich girl in Coín, and not a poor girl from Mijas?" Paca asked as she came out of the kitchen wiping her hands on her tattered apron. "Your mother liked me but she wasn't so happy that I became your *novia*. Your father was pleased, but not your mother…not until years later." Her broad smile was full of good natured humor as she reminded Paco of their shared history.

"Do you have memories of the Civil War?" I asked Paco during another of our languid Sundays at the *finca*.

"*Sí, sí, recuerdo los aviones arrojando bombas,*" he replied. "It was a terrible time and I remember it well. I was about eleven years old and the sound of the bombers overhead, dropping their bombs, was terrifying—out here in the *campo* we had nowhere to hide. My mother used to cover my eyes with her apron and put her hands tightly over my ears; she'd press me close to her so I wouldn't be frightened. Even so, I was very afraid. I was too young to go to war and my father's unit was never called up, but I remember some of my older cousins who went off to fight for the Republic and didn't come back. The family never heard what happened to them. A terrible time," he said, letting the solemnity of his memories hang heavily in the sultry summer air. It was one of the few times that Paco's merry heart turned somber.

Paco's brother Antonio, the oldest of Paco's three brothers, was a single man who never married; he shared the family life and all the hard labor of the fields with his brother. Antonio was tall and skinny compared to Paco, who was short and solid; Antonio was as quiet as his brother was lively. During the long hot days of summer and especially during the harvest there were no rest days at the *finca*. When Marshall came out to help gather the harvest, he and Antonio would sleep in the small storeroom where they kept the garlic and onions. Antonio was a heavy snorer and they all loved to laugh about the morning Marshall described how between snores Antonio fell completely silent. "I lay there in the dark," he told them, "afraid that Antonio had died in his sleep. Is he dead? I asked myself. Until Antonio's next snore."

Antonio and Francisco

Even on Sundays they labored. The two brothers and their straw hats could always be found bent double in the fields, planting or harvesting onions, garlic and tomatoes that they sold at the central produce market in Coín. One morning Antonio didn't show up and Paco went searching. He found that his brother had fallen into an *alberca*, a small pond on one of the neighboring *fincas*, and drowned.

The next time we visited Paca told me the sad news. "*¿Qué podemos hacer?*" Paco asked rhetorically, his calloused palms spread open in resignation.

Paca confided in me one afternoon that every night Paco would puzzle over Antonio's strange drowning: "*¿Cómo fue possible? ¿Es qué él se desmayó y cayó? ¿Es qué alguien malo le ha empujadó?* How is it possible? Was he dizzy and fell in? Did someone bad push him?" They never discovered the reason for Antonio's strange and untimely death. But the sadness and sense of loss hung like a dark shadow over the *finca*.

More Moroccan Mysteries

Reason is a light which is certainly needed to illuminate the darkness, but it can also be useful in full daylight.

— Mohammed Abed al-Jabri

O n this visit we floated into the Port of Tangier as a party of seven: Lauren and Marshall, eight and eleven, their diminutive and elegant grandmother from London, Sylvia Cohen, my mother-in-law, who brought all her party frocks along in her luggage. We were accompanied by Percy Seitlin and his wife, Alice, who were now spending half of every year as our neighbors in Fuengirola. Their granddaughter, Jennifer, who was Lauren's age and visiting from New York, was also joining us for a Moroccan adventure.

Sylvia, the London grandma, was a youthful sixty something who loved to change her clothes at least three times a day, and thus her suitcase was large and cumbersome. I am ashamed to admit that I practiced tough love, refusing to help her carry her bags. So she struggled away gamely lugging her baggage, until Marshall, who wisely ignored my mean-spirited injunctions, intervened. "Grandma," he said, let me carry that for you."

Lauren, Marshall, Zohar, Josef and Jennifer

Sylvia was all of four feet ten inches and on the uneven cobblestone streets of Tangier she tottered along in her high heels, at times one or the other of her feet slipping off the back of her open-toed shoes. She never complained, never stopped changing her dresses, and never stopped wearing high heels. I bless her memory for all the love and laughter that she brought into our lives.

I suppose it was because we were American friends of Naphtali Bensimon that we were all invited to be guests on Saturday night at the home of Tangier's chief of police. By now I had visited so often and seen so many odd things, that a dinner invitation to the home of the chief of police was just another…curiosity.

It all began well enough with smiles and introductions in Spanish and a little English since none of us spoke fluent French and the chief spoke only a smattering of English. The chief had a massive aquarium in his living room filled with neon-colored fish; it was clearly his pride and joy. He turned almost apoplectic when Marshall made the boyish mistake of putting his face close and placing his hands on the glass. The moment became nearly explosive with tension; Sylvia and I later agreed that we could almost feel the air move as he restrained himself, just in time, from smacking my young son across the room.

After some polite but awkward conversation, the chief's wife served couscous, scurrying in and out attending to us. She was never introduced, never sat down and never joined in the conversation. It was a rather remarkable if not mysterious experience.

Later Percy and I speculated: What did an Orthodox Jewish fortune-teller do to generate a dinner invitation from the chief of police of Tangier? What was their relationship? Neither of us could come up with a plausible explanation. I couldn't help but notice the strange nature of the goings-on of Naphtali Bensimon, but there was no one to ask but Solomon. I didn't want to embarrass him or put him on the spot, so I didn't ask.

While in Tangier we would always eat at small street restaurants where the *chilaba*-gowned men of the city ate. There was a particular soup—*hareera*—that the Moroccans used to break the fast each evening during the 28 days of Ramadan. At sundown a cannon's boom was heard throughout the city announcing the end of the fast. The first mouthful of food is always *hareera*. It was my pleasure to introduce Sylvia, Percy, Alice and Jennifer to the foods the children and I had come to love: I adored that thick soup of garbanzos, rice and tomatoes, and the fat rounds of whole wheat bread, warm and aromatic from the oven, that tasted equally delicious.

They were all willing adventurers and joined us in eating fluffy couscous and lamb kebabs pulled off the skewer and wrapped in hunks of delicious bread. As always, we finished the meal with mint tea so sweet it made my teeth ache. Nevertheless, we all loved the mint tea ritual: the waiters would hold the silver teapot packed to the lid with fresh mint high above their heads and pour the steaming green liquid in one long continuous stream to the delicate gold-rimmed glasses below. The fragrance of mint mixed with the steam of boiling water and sugar would perfume the air. In a city rife with mystery, it was certainly no mystery why most Moroccans, young and old, had large black holes in their front teeth. The enamel had been eaten away by sugary mint tea.

The streets of the old town—the *medina*—reeked with the combined smells of cumin, urine and burning charcoal. I loved that sharp, pungent fragrance but noted that it held less allure for Sylvia. I also loved the sounds of the *muezzin* calling the faithful to prayer from the top of the mosque's *minaret*. Five times each day his voice would ring out, float on the air awhile and wrap us in the cloak of its mournful beauty.

During our visits we would often stop by to greet the *shamus* of the old synagogue, and this time we went to introduce him to Sylvia, Percy, Alice and Jennifer, and to show them the wonderful old remnant of what had once been a robust and thriving Jewish community. A pious Jewish man always covers his head; when the *shamus* left the synagogue, he always replaced his yarmulke with a little gray fedora. I have an old black and white photograph of him, taken from the rear, with his small hat perched on his head with Lauren and Marshall, one on each side, his hands resting affectionately and protectively on their shoulders as they walked through the streets of Tangier. I also took many photographs of Marshall, Lauren and Percy up on the *bima* in that ancient Sephardic synagogue. Little could I have guessed that it would be the last time we would see the *shamus* or stand inside that beautiful and sacred ancient place.

That visit of our full entourage lasted just a few short days, but I felt certain that Percy, Alice and Sylvia were as enchanted, and mystified, as we were with the Bensimon family and as seduced by the mysteries and exotic spell cast over us by the gleaming white city of Tangier. Over the years we knew them, the kids and I, and once or twice Malcolm, made many trips to visit the Bensimons.

During one of our last visits, Naphtali announced that he was divorcing Coty and that she would be taking Tamo and going to Israel to live with her family in Beersheva. It was hard to tell for certain, but since he'd never shown much affection for her, he now seemed almost buoyant that he was getting rid of her—like the pleasure of driving away a pest. I felt sad for Coty because she would be leaving behind both of her boys; Naphtali would never allow her to take his sons. I knew that her life with Naphtali could not have been easy. But through it all she just kept silently smiling.

Understanding dimly that our visits would be coming to an end and that their family as we had known it would not be the same, I asked Solomon if we could visit the old synagogue once again. He told me that the roof had fallen in and it was now merely a pile of rubble. All those beautiful silver lamps, all that history, crushed in the dust; it was painful to imagine. We didn't even get to say a proper goodbye to the old *shamus* who had always welcomed us so graciously and cared for the old synagogue so proudly.

MAKING LIMONADA

Rejoneadora

And God took a handful of southerly wind, blew
His breath over it and created the horse.

— Bedouin legend

I n southern Spain, among the rich at least, no one takes things too seriously. Omnipresent business deals and the state of one's testicles are matters to be approached fairly casually and not allowed to seriously impinge on eating, drinking and wringing the last drop of goodness from each day. It's that Spanish mastery of continually tapping into the effervescence of life that so seduces foreigners.

By contrast, everything I did at that time had an intensity and fervor to it that had to be exhausting to my family—particularly my riding. I was a zealot, practicing hour after hour, until the midday sun pressed its own not-to-be-ignored intensity on the land. Then hot, dusty and often ragged with frustration, I'd head home and drop into exhausted sleep.

Somewhere in those years I had become obsessed with the need to confront my own mortality, test my courage, look death in the eye and laugh. Early mornings I'd walk to the stables, whispering to myself and to the empty streets: "Please help me face this test with dignity and calm, no matter what." Now the day I had been preparing for was galloping toward me at full speed through the dust.

Training with Favorito to face the bulls

The months of preparation and training were over. The many nights spinning dizzily into headachy dawns of too much Tio Pepe and La Ina. Nights of too much laughter and camaraderie, endless cigarettes, till my throat and nostrils were numb. My strained smile, and the effort it took to maintain it, had taken a toll. I am by nature serious, and in the fun-loving crowd of wealthy Spanish men with whom Malcolm and I hung out, serious was not allowed. In countless bars around town, a thick carpet of prawn and lobster shells lay crunched under the heels of countless handmade boots. This expensive detritus paid homage to my companions and backers, these sated princes of Andalucía. To these men I represented novelty and a curious mixture of intensity, machismo and femininity. And I, a young wife and mother of four, wanted to live as carefree and robustly as they did. They were giving me an unusual chance for a woman and a foreigner: the chance to test my courage and skill in the *rejoneo*, the artful bullfight from horseback. In this centuries-old sport of the royalty of Spain and Portugal, finely trained horses of great beauty and speed wear no protective padding; their safety depends entirely on their rider's skill and judgment. Yet I was so intent on proving myself to myself that I didn't even notice the double-edged quality of their gift: my test, their entertainment. Pride and arrogance, like the viscous sweet Málaga wine, had gone to my head. We would use each other well.

Outside the bullring, dark Mercedes disgorged rotund bankers, ranchers in suits and boots and gentlemen playboys from as far west as the perpetually foggy province of Cadiz. The day's spectacle would be presided over by patriarch Don José Quesada, who, in honor of the occasion, had donated three-year-old fighting bulls from his breeding ranch. Wide brimmed sombrero Cordobeses bobbed above long, expensive, Monte Cristo Cuban cigars, and made their way in a crush to their seats. Two of Spain's top matadors would be with me in the ring—just in case. A mammoth fig tree provided dappled shade. Wine and tapas flowed—tulip-shaped glasses of sherry, plates of grilled pork loin, manchego cheese and pale green *manzanilla* olives—all to whet the appetite for the spectacle to come.

My boots were new, hand made, and rubbed lightly on my inner calf. That morning, after I had dressed, I had been pleased and proud of my reflection in the dimpled old glass of the doors to our patio. Blond hair tied back with a black satin ribbon set off my short black jacket with its velvet collar; the white lace front of my shirt and cuffs were starched and stiff. Pinstriped, body-hugging trousers rose high at my waist. They were a little slack, since the kilos had melted away in the course of preparing for the day. My leather chaps—*zahones*— had been hand made for me in Sevilla and hand sewn with white catgut, with my initials inscribed on the wide band at my waist. Those supple zahones would protect my legs from a dangerous slice by the bull's razor sharp horns. The horses had no protection other than my skill. All those trappings had mattered that morning as I carefully placed my pale-gray *sombrero* Cordobes on my head. None of it mattered later. What mattered later was the safety of the horses, managing their fear and my own and the bull. No amount of imagining had prepared me for facing a *toro bravo*, but no matter what happened, I was determined to not falter in fear.

A big van with the horses had arrived hours before— $20,000 worth of sleek Spanish stallions, hauled in an open produce truck. Favorito, my big white steed with his majestic head and noble heart, stood saddled and bridled. His mane was braided with red and yellow satin ribbons, the colors of the Spanish flag. He was impatient and restlessly pawed the ground with one front hoof. Pepe the Horse hissed a threat: "caballooo." The pawing stopped obediently. In addition to Favorito I was to ride a dappled-gray, Cancionero, I knew less well. Because of the terrible tension the horses experience with a charging bull, they tire quickly and must be changed often. Eighteen-year-old Díablo, quick to throw any rider who dared tug on his mouth, glowed bronze-red in the sunlight. On those three my life would depend, and their safety and security rested in my hands; a delicate, fragile thread of trust ran between us.

I wandered away for a few minutes alone and discovered a whitewashed wall where I could peer down into dark, curious eyes. The bulls had smooth muscled shoulders and almost perfect crescent curves of horn. Handsome young creatures, not yet in their prime. And despite the brilliant sun on my back, I felt a cold quietness descend over my body and mind, felt myself move to another arena where I could not be touched.

I swung up into the saddle as the gates of the ring opened; Don Antonio Albion, my trainer and a skilled *rejoneador*, led the way. I sat tall and firmly rooted to Favorito as we cantered into the ring. The certainty that we made a stunning pair was my last thought as I caught a glimpse of red capes and the matadors pressed back against the barriers at the ready. And then, almost as a shock, I saw him across the sand: the bull, dark and coiled explosively. Suddenly a sledge-hammer started pounding my chest, obstructing my breath. My eardrums thundered and heart fluttered wildly, terrified wingbeats trapped in netting. Was it possible that one heavy, black *toro bravo* could cover the distance across the ring in the blink of an eye? Yet there he was! I couldn't remember which leg to press against Favorito to swerve him left, out of the way of those deadly horns. Through thick cotton I head Pepe's voice yelling instructions…"*Doña* Diana, *muévase a la izquierda, aprieta las piernas…*" It was a language I didn't understand. Why couldn't I think? I was a tangle of unresponsive hands and contradictory calves, witlessly urging my horse into the path of the bull, rather than pivoting safely away. For one moment that lasted an eternity, my heart stopped, as Favorito received the full force of the dark mass on his right flank. Horrified, I quickly scanned for blood but thankfully saw none. My horse, my beloved Favorito…what had I done? Despite a blow that could have eviscerated him had the bull hooked up with those lethal horns, we survived the first act. Cautiously we cantered in wide turns around the bull, keeping our distance, as I now knew the explosive speed with which it could move. (At short distances the *toro bravo* is faster than a horse I learned later.) Favorito, who so willingly and trustingly carried me into battle, was lathered with sweat. I could hear Pepe shouting that I had to switch horses. It would take Favorito many weeks to recover his spirit and health, many weeks before I could ride him again. I had ruptured the fragile thread of trust with the horse I loved best.

As I remounted Díablo someone thrust a *banderilla* up to my hands. One end was covered in white crepe paper, the other was a sharp steel hook. I was supposed to ride in close enough that I could lean down and thrust the steel point hard into the bull's thick neck, just behind the horns. Then the horse and I were to pirouette away. Had I ever tried this? Had anyone explained this fine detail? Yet I was so game that I grabbed the *banderilla* obediently, willing to give it a go. But I wasn't the only novice being tested that day. None of the horses had ever faced a bull. I had rehearsed many of those moves a million times in my imagination yet I simply did not have the skills to come in that close. Or was it lack of nerve? I hadn't faltered in fear but I hadn't come close to laughing either. Somehow the only blood spilled that morning was that of the bull. One of the matadors, Miguel Marquez, killed him, a task I had not been trained to do.

Lunch was a celebration. Long tables had been laid with white linens on the terrace above the plaza. Bread, olives, almost transparent slices of *jamon serrano*, and platters of green salad glistened with olive oil: a celebration and a feast!

White-jacketed waiters carried in the main course: huge pans of golden hued paella. One of the promoters had brought along the cooks and waiters from his hotel along the seafront. I ate almost nothing but gulped down cold white wine to still my trembling hands. And the wine flowed, followed by coffee and cognac and, of course, more Havana cigars.

Lunch was a celebration   Mike Lewin photo

Then the second half of the day unfolded: taking up the heavy crimson cape and meeting another bull, this time on foot. The dust in the ring was thick and deep. One needed to be light of foot to even move in it. All the hours spent with the cape to strengthen my wrist, and all the passes I had practiced over and over again facing a stuffed bull's head on a single wheel...all that experience and so much more I needed now. With my head floating from too much wine and too little food, I stood in the ring, cape in hand, tall, erect, alone—what Juan Belmonte, one of Spain's most beloved *matadores*, called "an unimaginable loneliness." I called the bull to me. "*Je je toro.*" My voice came out sure and steady. And he came—so fast, so direct, that I had no time to move. Instead of passing neatly through the outstretched cape he tossed me and luckily mowed me down. I say luckily, because it might have been otherwise. It might have been his horn in my gut. Temporarily drawn off by the matadors, the bull's attention was deflected and I scrambled to my feet without the good sense to be shaking. I grabbed the dusty cape, and with legs firmly rooted to the sand, called him to me with all the arrogance I could muster. But my feet were clumsy and leaden, and I couldn't seem to move them. Twice I got up for more until on the third try, I could see his eyes looking not at the cape, but dead center at my torso. That time he not only tossed me but caught my head with one of his hoofs and I went down for the count. I recalled little more than lashing out with one spurred boot in furious frustration. The next thing I remembered was being carried from the ring protesting, and having cold water sloshed unceremoniously over my head, without regard for the velvet collar. Perhaps the fun had gone too far.

It was only sometime later that I learned I should have been warned to take off my spurs as they impede quick movements in the thick dust. The rest was a blur. I vaguely recall the offer of another fight, then home and bed. Weeks followed when I'd jolt awake from a deep sleep seeing the piercing, intelligent eyes of that bull focused squarely on my body. I had come to know fear intimately.

The details of returning a second time to the ring—without Favorito—for another, less feted, attempt are dim. All the arrogance and bravado in which I had cloaked myself protectively, had been stripped away. I have an old black and white photo of me, jaw clenched in rigid determination, mid-air on Cancionero as we jumped the body of the prostrate bull. I had faced the bulls and bested my fear, but there was no winner. Not me, not the horses and certainly not the bulls. I learned I didn't want to kill bulls, didn't want to snuff out their magnificent power.

Mike Lewin photo

Later I would come to hate seeing the fierce majesty of the *toro bravo* reduced to a lifeless dark mass, prostrate in the dust. The nightmares of a riderless white stallion about to be gored in the bullring intensified. Always it was the same white stallion—Favorito—always facing death. I would wake sobbing, the tears soaking my pillow.

We all test our courage in different ways. I did what I did at that moment because I was offered the chance. But didn't I realize that long ago morning, as I sent my children off to school, that by risking my life with the bulls, they could lose their mother? Did I really not see the risk of dealing them another terrible loss? Such a recognition only came later.

Besides, in my entire life there had never been anyone telling me no, least of all Malcolm. And I probably wouldn't have listened even if he had tried. By undertaking this risky challenge I had thought only of myself as if the people who loved me didn't deserve an opinion or my children didn't deserve the security of knowing their mother would be there to see them grow up. As it was, I was a law unto myself.

Meltdown

The mind is its own place and in itself can make
a Heav'n of Hell
or a Hell of Heav'n.

— Satan, John Milton's *Paradise Lost*

There may be a better description of what was happening to me than Milton's words. If so, they do not come to mind.

I never heard the hours of my life ticking away. I had successfully, albeit unconsciously, numbed myself to the pain and guilt that roiled below the surface, yet depression still dropped like a cloak around me; I didn't have the skills to push it away and fight it enveloping me in its thick, heavy folds.

It happened suddenly, but the warning signs had been there all along: The recurring nightmare of the white stallion about to be gored in the bullring—always facing death. Dark dreams of stumbling on my mother, murdered by the father I had never known, who then killed himself. For weeks my pillow was soggy; I would be startled awake by ghastly scenes I tried to escape, and spent my days exhausted from the nighttime horrors. All the unresolved conflicts and abandonment by my mother on a freezing November night churned within. There was the grief that I had never allowed myself to feel over Mark dying so suddenly, angry rage at his abandonment and guilt that I had in some way been responsible. Even Mark's parents had disappeared, leaving me to stumble blindly without guidance; now his mother referred to me as "living a transient life." (Proper women, especially wives and mothers, didn't have adventures and move around the world, for heaven's sake.) But somewhere in those years of running away from my own story, I had run away from myself. Without a sense of self, I had nothing to give to the people who loved me. Sometimes I wanted to die to escape the pain. Other times I would have compromised by remaining in the blessed oblivion of sleep. But asleep or awake, the pain was always there, lurking in the shadows.

Malcolm tried to help and be supportive but I sensed his impotence and that frightened me. For example: we were invited to go to Marbella to visit some wealthy friends of his who were on holiday from London. I experienced complete paralysis at the thought of spending the day with his sophisticated London friends. I had nothing to wear, and felt so emotionally and mentally bankrupt that the stress of even imagining the need to make intelligent conversation and be "on" for others, as in the light bulb, required more fortitude than I felt I possessed. Malcolm tried his best. He walked me across the patio to the bathroom and had me stand in front of the mirror. He urged me to say to my reflection "you are a good person and a good human being." Or words to that effect. The face that looked back at me was scrunched up with anguish; although I dimly appreciated the aid he was trying to offer to my listing ship.

I couldn't see the truth of my life, rich beyond measure: four bright and healthy youngsters, a husband who loved being Boy Scout leader to his "five" children, a rambling and gracious old home just blocks from the sea, pets and horses, good health, good looks, youth. I had it all. But when depression and never ending sadness take hold, the battle becomes a fight for one's very life. That was my fight and I wanted to lose. I used to walk down our street thinking about the millions of people who were dying and how desperately they wanted to live. Yet I had a life that I found so painful I wanted it to end. It seemed grotesquely funny.

Sometimes it is the kindness of strangers that makes all the difference. An American named Sally Lindover, visiting from the East Coast of the U.S., was staying in town and had become a friend. Sally had been trained as a therapist and saw my deep distress. She offered to take me with her back to London and deposit me into the hands of an outstanding American psychologist, Dr. Daniel R. Miller, who had been practicing in London for a number of years. And she did.

Sally found me a place to stay and arranged that I would have a therapy session with Dan Miller every day for three months. And thus began one of the most intensely painful but ultimately liberating investments in my own mental and emotional strength. I thank Sally for having been my guardian angel. Like in the bullring, it might have been otherwise.

In those early months I hated Dan Miller. He was about 50 years old, which I took to be very old, and he was brutal and shockingly blunt. He didn't give a damn if I cried my eyes out at the realities he pointed out. My carefully thought-out rationale for fleeing to Spain was just a cover up to keep from facing the fact that I had run away from disastrous relationships: my first marriage, and the resulting overwhelming responsibilities, isolation and loneliness I had felt, and with my mother and my mother-in-law. At some unconscious level I felt so guilty that I believed I deserved their harsh judgements. I had, he asserted, chosen the emptiness of Fuengirola, a place that reflected the emptiness and worthlessness I felt inside. While my future training and education should have been my number one priority, I pushed those realities away and filled my life with dangerous physical challenges that could bring more disaster into my children's lives. Dan Miller held up a mirror and forced me to take a hard look. What I saw was a woman who cared so little for her children that she was not thinking about their future or their education. I saw someone whose angry outbursts pushed away the people who loved her most. I was that woman and I was creating a massive wreckage of my life and the lives of what he called my children's "little souls." And I didn't give a damn but would go on obliviously dancing on the carnage strewn at my feet unless he, Dan Miller, put a stop to my tyranny. No wonder I didn't like myself and had been turning my anger against myself; there wasn't much to like.

I was self-centered, he told me, lacking awareness of those around me, unable to see them as individuals. If someone told me I was intelligent I could find ways of throwing away that knowledge. Didn't I want to dig down and discover my strengths, stand on my own feet and feel proud of myself? he asked. And over the weeks he threw back at me all the incriminating evidence of my worthlessness that I had so trustingly revealed. (There is a quote by a psychologist named C.A. Mace, written in the journal I kept at the time: "We might be a little more exacting in our demand for proof of our own incompetence." Clearly my spirit and Dr. Miller were engaged in battle.) Despite fighting him every step of the way, arguing with his pronouncements, telling him "I hate you," once I started to take a hard, unemotional look at the Truth of My Life as written by Dr. Dan Miller, I started to regain my equilibrium. How can something so brutal be transforming? It is a mystery. Dan Miller also helped me to see another possible explanation for my mother's desertion after Mark's death: She, who had had to raise me alone and without resources, may have been overwhelmed by seeing history repeat itself. Her daughter would now be raising not one child but three all alone. It may have been too much for her to bear. I found that strangely healing; rather than anger I could feel compassion for my mother's pain.

During those long months alone in London I had plenty of time for self-reflection: I gained some insight into the non-verbal contract that Malcolm and I had made early in our relationship: a little girl/daddy set up. I began to acknowledge the rage and depression I felt when he short changed me emotionally, and wasn't always the "good daddy," and how sometimes he wasn't home mentally or emotionally. The "contract" wasn't between two self-determined adults—the bargain cheated us both. I also began to recognize that the depressions I'd been feeling were trying to tell me something. I began to understand the recurring nightmare of the riderless white stallion always facing death: the horse, Favorito, represented the best parts of myself, my highest ideals and values, parts put at risk by the thoughtless and careless ways I lived. Carl Jung, I would learn, said it clearly: we ignore our dreams at our own peril.

Of course there were lots of missteps along the way, lots of one step forward and two or three backward. Yet I made a wonderful discovery: I had great emotional courage. Since I first discovered it in those awful months, I have loved that about myself. It's something to be proud of. I could face my truths and come out the other side determined to act differently and most importantly, to feel my children's "little souls."

One sunny morning months later, I was standing out in the patio of our house, appreciating all the lush foliage of the plants that Marshall had tended and watered so lovingly in my absence. Abruptly, Malcolm blurted out, "I liked you better the way you were before." For a moment I couldn't find my voice.

"You liked me better before? What was I like before? You liked me better when I was falling apart? What are you telling me?" My careful control spun up like my rising voice into the tops of the castor and banana trees that unfurled overhead, enveloping me in a haze of shock and disbelief. Some hope that we could make a better marriage started dying that morning.

Whether Malcolm liked me better the way I was before or not, I knew there was no going back. Not if I wanted to learn how to be a truly loving parent. Not if I wanted to live with pride and a sense of achievement. Not if I wanted to live with joy. And thus began the first day of the rest of my life.

Unraveling of a Life

Make dust our paper and with weeping eyes write
sorrow on the bosom of the earth.
— Shakespeare, *King Richard II*

Sundays and holidays are the loneliest days in a Spanish town. The streets are silent, the restaurants and bars overflow with multi-generational families. They swarm at tables laden with platters of crisp fish, green salads, icy bottles of Tio Pepe and foam-rimmed glasses of San Miguel beer. They talk with their hands, their eyebrows bob up and down. Their laughter and shouts billow out into the lonely streets. Spain is a happily boisterous country, but not if you're on the outside looking in. It is the same today as it was all those long years ago.

Once again I was alone with my children without a husband and they without their father. Why do marriages unravel? I have some ideas. I'm sure Malcolm has others. I thought it was over for me and that I could go it alone. The stresses had been many. Some were subtle and some not.

Because of the intense therapy in London, I could now confront the guilt I had felt over Mark's sudden death, begin to forgive my mother, and recognize my own loss of a compass. But digging in the dust of our buried memories can unwittingly invite them to rise, like frightening apparitions in the night. Knowing this helps me understand myself and how Spain too wanted only to forget: her past, the agonies of her Civil War and the terrible years of hunger, death squads and the repression that followed. I didn't want to remember either, but, like Spain, if I was to make peace with my history, I would have to find the courage to continue to dig deeply, take a long hard look and tolerate a time of turmoil.

Besides, the children were growing up. What was I going to do with my life? I'd always been aware of the dead-ended emptiness of the expat community, but exactly what I wanted for my life I didn't know. I just knew I wanted more.

One morning I was driving back from Málaga with my closest friend and neighbor, Patzi Gordon Davis.

"Diana, did you go to university?"

"Of course," I lobbed back without knowing enough to fake a school or a major. But the lie made me uneasy and told me a lot about myself. A kaleidoscope's blurred image began shifting into focus. In an abstract way I'd always wanted to go to university although nobody in my immediate family had done so. Mark became a father, then died before he had a chance for more education. Malcolm had gone to work at eighteen and had no college education. I was like a hungry kid looking through a window at a table laden with food, but my hunger was for a sense of achievement that would help me to feel proud.

Through Fuengirola's world of horses I had become friends with an older, aristocratic American lady who gave me all her books, her art and her typewriter when she moved back to the U.S. The books included volumes on art and philosophy, and by reading them I began to sense the heady realm of libraries and imagine discussions about psychology and philosophy. Where months before I had walked the streets of Fuengirola mired in a trough of sadness, now I was thinking about Freud's theories, Jung's dream symbols and the hauntingly poetic way that the naturalist, Loren Eisley, wrote about the earth. I could hear the musical cadence of Eisley's voice and know for sure that I wanted to write like he wrote. Because of my elderly friend's generosity, my world became the world of ideas in the pile of books that teetered on and under my desk: *Moses and Monotheism, Man and His Symbols*, and Conrad Lorenz's *King Solomon's Ring*. But I had no one who shared my interests. I had tried floating serious conversations once or twice at Bar La Cepa and had driven away whomever it was I was talking to. Clearly a good cocktail conversationalist I was not.

You'd have thought that my intense loneliness would have driven me deeper into my children's lives, that I could have derived satisfaction from their rapidly evolving selves. But I wasn't yet mature enough to see them as complex and interesting people worthy of my absorption. Besides, I was focused on finding myself yet wasn't sure where to look. All that would start to come later. Someone once said that we'd best grow up before our children do. In my case we were all growing up together.

Still, the seeds of a parent who could feel her children's "little souls" had been planted as a result of the therapy. I was even beginning to imagine a future beyond Fuengirola. Because of the depth of the work I'd been doing with Dan Miller, I was alternating between feeling vulnerable and bewildered, yet more often self-directed, calm and steady. I was feeling adequate to life.

I also felt enormous gratitude to Malcolm. He had come into our lives at a time when I was still reeling from the shock of Mark's death. Malcolm assumed the responsibility of marrying me and being father to my young children, a burden very few men would have been willing to undertake. I'd married Mark when I was nineteen, had Lisa when I was barely twenty, David less than a year later, and a few short years later, Mark was killed when I was newly pregnant with Marshall. So I'd never really had a late adolescence free of responsibilities. As tragic as it was that Mark's young life was snuffed out, that he'd never see his children grow up nor his children know their father, the reality is that his death gave me a chance to start my life over.

I don't know for sure what Malcolm saw in my children and me but we were certainly a ready-made family. Because he was such a natural "mother" he stepped into our lives and took over the role of being both parents. He allowed me the freedom to have that adolescence I'd never had. But the problem was I was now ready to assume the responsibilities of an adult and, as he said, he liked me "better the way I was before."

It can't have been easy being married to me. Interesting but not easy. But no one wears a totally black hat in a marriage, not even me. However, I'm not sure I understood that at the time.

"Why do you always have to be hurling yourself against a brick wall?" Malcolm would ask laughing. "Why do you always have to be striving for something? Why can't you just be content? I think it's because it must feel so good when you stop," he'd joke. Ask the cat to change its spots. Now I see he was pointing out our differences. I'd be tackling personal challenges until I was a hundred, always seeking out the next once while he was polishing the jokes in his repertoire so he could hold court and be the life of any party or the expert on any topic of conversation.

About this time I had spied a flyer announcing that the *ayuntamiento* was sponsoring a summer session of intensive, advanced Spanish classes. I don't remember the cost, but we could have managed. I must have sought Malcolm's approval, although God knows I never asked it for anything else. But I was trying to mend my ways and learn new habits, like talking over decisions with my husband. In any case, he was opposed and even made light-hearted jest of me wanting to be a student, saying it was too much money that we couldn't afford. He wasn't interested himself, content to let his bubbly humor cover any errors in style. In the early years not speaking much Spanish allowed me to hide away. Now I craved fluency and mastery of the complicated verb tenses. I didn't want to be one of the town's many *extranjeros* who, despite years of residency, cranked up the volume of their voices to compensate for their lack of vocabulary. We had always chuckled about it when we heard them·

"I say *por favor*, dame that one *aqui*."

Even though I knew that studying Spanish would be good for me, shifting me into *ratio* and away from the vortex of emotions, Malcolm was treating me like a child. His lack of support had a severe chilling effect. But strangely I caved in and it didn't serve me or our marriage well.

There was also the ongoing power struggle over my desk: It was just a rickety table piled unsteadily with books, calligraphy tools, journals with my prose and poetry, and the detritus of someone who loved writing, papers and pens.

"Why do you need your own desk?" Malcolm would chide me. "Why can't you be better about sharing?" He made it sound like there was something wrong with me for wanting a small space of my own. Not yet recognizing that he had a problem respecting boundaries, I partially believed him.

It's the little things, like our ongoing struggles over my independence, that help me understand how I could have been so certain our marriage was over. One day we drove 220 miles on very narrow country roads to the American Consulate in Sevilla so Malcolm could renew the green card that would allow him to live and work in California. He was still a British subject. Then we turned around and drove back to Fuengirola. It was a hard drive in more ways than just the hours. We didn't talk much. What was there to say that hadn't already been said? Regardless of what it seemed like to him, it wasn't easy for me to tell him our marriage was over. Did I think about the destabilizing effect this separation would have on our children? Did I imagine that Lauren would feel abandoned? If I did, I must have had some way of rationalizing it. Children know when their parents are unhappy.

One morning the children and I drove Malcolm to Málaga airport and said good-bye. There had to have been a lot of tears and sadness but I don't remember. Lauren tells me that she didn't even know her dad was leaving for good until she saw me start to cry at the airport. Did I think that the less the children knew the less painful and confusing Malcolm's departure would be? Clearly I felt so guilty about the decision being my responsibility that I couldn't even explain it to them, either before he left or after.

Long faces, a suddenly quiet house, yet I felt a sense of relief. In the following weeks Lauren started being particularly naughty. One afternoon, when I attempted to turn her over my knee for a quick swat on her rear end, her screams and shrieks reverberated through the house. You'd have thought I was about to kill her. Lisa started staying out late with Humberto, her *novio*, her first boyfriend. No amount of pleading and negotiating her return hour worked reliably. Each evening she'd promise to be home on time but the hour would come and go while I waited expectantly out in the dark street. I'd get madder and madder and Lisa would grow increasingly sullen and resentful. There was no resolution.

One night when Lisa wasn't home long after the time we'd agreed on, I drove to Humberto's family estate in Los Boliches. I pushed open the high iron gates and called her name. Two Dobermans came tearing at me through the dark, barking and snarling, their rage a leaping fireball of fury. Just in time I pulled the heavy gate closed as they hurled themselves again and again against it. I could have been torn apart by those dogs. I stood there in the night shaking with fear and shock, furious with my daughter.

Weeks later I was scorching under the hair dryer in Rosendo's *peluquería*, the homely hairdressing salon down around the corner, when Lisa burst through the door with a ghostly pale David, his hand wrapped in a bloody towel.

"Mom, David cut his hand using the electric saw." Dr. Verdugo's office was just across the street; mercifully the nurse showed us right in. The doctor was aptly named as it turned out. The *verdugo* is the executioner. Without a shot to numb David's pain, Dr. Verdugo threaded a curved needle and proceeded to sew up the deep gash in the fleshy part of David's thumb. He sank in that needle, then pulled it out the other side, while I squeezed my son's other hand as though I could drain away some of the hurt. His body convulsed with each jab of the needle. Butcher. Why didn't I demand an anesthetic for my boy? In those days, in that culture, one did not question the doctor. The *médico* was like God.

When did I realize that we'd always be *extranjeros*, foreigners? Spain wasn't like the U.S. where foreigners melt rather easily into the texture of the culture. Years before I thought I had found in this village and this country the embracing family I needed. Now I had outgrown it and was beginning to see its faults and realize that part of the emptiness I felt inside came from being an expat in an empty world of expats. As a foreigner I wouldn't be able to become involved in town politics or take any role in the growing city's planning. As a foreigner I didn't have the right to have my voice heard and express my opinions. It was still a strict dictatorship and a patriarchal society. Yet I was starting to recognize that I had a voice, opinions, and a good brain that needed to be engaged in more than just living from day to day.

Lisa, Marshall and Coco making paella

About this time, in a surprising gesture of bridge-building, my mother sent us a care package of tins of sardines and thick-sliced bacon with the rind on it—the way I'd loved it as a child. What my mother didn't know was that Spain was not only the cradle of pork but the land of sardines. However, the affection the package expressed was healing and a step forward.

One afternoon the heavy pounding of the iron door-knocker assaulted the quiet of our house. A pair of olive-green garbed *Guardía Civil* stood rigidly at the door, their expressions funereal. They took my fifteen-year-old David away, marching him down the street, one on either side holding his elbow. I wasn't *bien enchufado*, well connected—everything in Spain is about your connections—and I didn't know where to turn. So I did the next best thing. It was a hot afternoon but I put on my rabbit fur coat to convey to the *Guardía* that I was a woman of means to be dealt with. I squared my broad shoulders and marched the few blocks to their *cuartel*, their headquarters, breathing fire and brimstone, my heart galloping, my hands thrust into my pockets to hide their flutter.

"What has he done that he deserves being arrested?" I demanded. "He's only a boy, my eldest son, an excellent student...*un buen chico. Estoy orgulloso de él.* He's a good boy and I'm proud of him," I asserted. The words tumbled out without regard for the *Guardía's* omnipotence.

"*Señora, alguien ha denunciado su hijo...*"

Annonomous denuciations were still a somber reality of life in a Spanish village. A neighbor had denounced David to the *Guardía* for climbing over the wall that separated our patio from one of the houses behind when he'd gone to retrieve a ball he'd been tossing around. Neighbors didn't just come around the corner to let you know that your kid had come into their garden and to please, next time, knock on the door. Instead they denounced him and had him arrested. Such was the surveillance society we lived in. Such was the frighteningly swift retribution of the *Guardía Civil* for a boy's minor infraction. They let him go but the situation had terrified me.

That night I had another nightmare. In the dream David had been arrested for breaking the window of a *tienda*, a tiny shop on the corner. Malcolm was standing with his back to me, not moving. Marshall was screaming, "Mom, come quickly, they've got David." I raced down the street but arrived too late. The *Guardía Civil* had hanged him. My first instinct was to blow breath into his lifeless body but I realized I was too late. I was swept by despair. The haunting words of King David who discovered his son hanging from an oak tree by his long blond hair infiltrated my dream:

"Oh Absalom, my beloved son Absalom!"

The dangerous wound with the electric saw, the shocking arrest by the *Guardía Civil* and David hanged in my nightmare: It's like it was all preparing me for the morning David said, "Mom, I want to go back to live in California with Malcolm." Intellectually I knew that he'd be better off finishing high school in California. He'd have better chances for good colleges. Even though Lisa and both boys attended St. Anthony's College, an English college preparatory school, the hybrid kids who grew up in Spain, but weren't Spanish, floundered. I dimly understood that he was making a smart choice for his future yet I was starting to feel slightly numb with loss. So one day we drove David to Málaga airport. The rent in the fabric of our lives that began when Malcolm left was unraveling. Now we were four.

Land of Milk and Honey

Every man under his vine and fig tree and none
shall be afraid.

— Micah 4.4

I do believe the universe looks out for us. My friend Ann Karren, at whose Passover Seder I had met Malcolm, was now married and living in Israel. Ann wrote that an Israeli friend would be coming to Spain and she had given her friend Elli my name. Elli, a girl, right? One Sunday morning the children and I were eating garlic toast and *churros* in a bar around the corner, when a ginger-haired man walked in, stuck out his hand and said, "Hello, I'm Elli."

Elli Nachlieli, a Tel Aviv photographer and filmmaker, stayed with us for a week and blew a breath of invigorated air into all our lives. He artfully photographed the children and me, told us stories about the founding of the state of Israel and promised to send me books on Israel's history. We bonded with him immediately: Marshall and Elli over their mutual passion for photography, Lauren and Lisa because he was sort of a kid himself, and me because he was smart, funny and just good company.

Lisa   Elli Nachlieli photo

It is because of Elli that my interest in Israel blossomed. When he was back home he sent me a couple of books and I started reading and dreaming. So it wasn't surprising that I began to devise the one strategy at which I excelled, the one that had served me well in the past: I began planning an adventure, and in this case, an exploration of Israel.

I still couldn't face the prospect of returning to live in California, yet I knew that we had all outgrown our life in Spain. So I made arrangements for Lauren to stay with the family of one of her school pals. And I asked our *señora*, our maid who came in daily, to shop and cook for Lisa and Marshall during my absence. What made it OK for me to think I could go off and leave them to look after themselves? I have to remind myself that it was a small town and a different era. Besides, they were sixteen and twelve, I must have reasoned. Maybe if I found us a new place to live—Israel— everything would turn out all right. Like a frantic swimmer desperate for breath, I was searching for a lifeline into the future.

A month or so later I flew alone to London and then on to Israel. Would Israel be a good place for us to live? Would the country provide a sense of meaning that had been lost in our lives? I returned after two weeks thoroughly besotted with the idealism and energy I had felt there. Israel was certainly a place for dreams of a better life. It was a country that had been founded on courage against all odds. Elli took me to Acre prison where his uncle, Dov Gruner, had been hanged by the British High Commission in 1947 for being a member of the Irgun, what the British called a terrorist group, fighting for a Jewish homeland.

Bob Cohn, Ann's cousin from the Seder, took me to stay on Kibbutz Hanita, on the Lebanese border. After midnight, unable to sleep, I stood on the balcony of my room in softly falling rain, looking out towards where I judged Beirut to be, watching flashes of lightening illuminate the clouds pink and gray, the whole firmament rumbling with thunder. I heard machine gun fire in the hills and saw searchlights sweep the darkness. Earlier in the day I had noted a U.N. observation post visible in the distance. Lights on the fencing that surrounded the kibbutz turned the darkness phosphorescent white. Suddenly the lightening shorted out the floodlights and everything went black. It was unlike any experience I've ever had—a curious excitement laced with the tiniest bit of fear. The sound of Israeli army vehicles on patrol, and the sweep of their headlamps back and forth along the road below, was reassuring. Yet it seemed hard to believe that so much hostility existed so close at hand.

Lauren and Diana   Elli Nachlieli photo

In the communal dining room I raised my voice in singing *Hava Nagila*, the Israeli folksong, and joined a large circle of dancers for the *hora*. I keenly felt the radiance of kibbutz life and marveled at the young army members and kibbutzniks entering the dining room carrying their weapons and depositing them on a pile of coats in the corner.

Ann and Baruch at their Bedouin wedding,   Zev Radovan photo

I was in Israel for Yom Kippur with Ann and her husband, the documentary filmmaker, Baruch Gitlis, and their young daughter Sara. On the holiest day of the year the entire country shuts down. People flooded the streets and we walked together, arm in arm, as a community of Jews. I felt part of a family again and was intoxicated with the Jewish homeland, the core value of right conduct and the richness of intellectual life and love of the land. It was a young country literally flowing, at least as I saw it then, with milk and honey, a wonderful country for children.

On November 20, 1975, I read in the Jerusalem Post that Spain's dictator, *Generalísimo* Francisco Franco y Bahamonde, *el Caudillo*, supreme head of state, had finally died. I say finally, because he had been dying for months, and had only been kept alive artificially under the orders of aging Fascist ideologues, fearful of what lay ahead. Spain was about to undergo enormous changes as the tightly controlled Franco era came to an end. Who knew what would happen? Chaos, another civil war, lawlessness in the streets? I saw in Spain's uncertain future a parallel with our own uncertain lives.

I also learned something else about Franco from reading the morning's news: Franco, long considered the pariah of Europe, was lauded by the Israelis for having refused to turn over to the Nazis those Jews who had made it safely to Spain. Apparently Franco never violated that safety net of sheltering Jews even when their persecution elsewhere in Europe was at its worst and Hitler's demands most strident.

I came home to Lisa, Marshall and Lauren, loaded with English tea and cheeses and made the most glorious Sunday morning breakfast. As we sat on the high stools around the red formica kitchen table, I started telling them the stories of survival that had been told to me. I described life on the *moshavim* and *kibbutzim*, the collective farms. I told them of a country of young soldiers, both men and women, not so very much older than they were...strong, sun-kissed young people dressed in military fatigues with rifles slung over their shoulders...young idealists all over the country.

"You absolutely have to see this amazing country. You will fall in love with Israel too," I promised.

Did I stop talking long enough to ask them how they were and how they had fared in my absence? And while I talked we ate Stilton cheese heaped on crisp cream crackers, drank big mugs of English tea with milk, and inhaled smoked salmon on piles of buttered toast. A glorious breakfast reunion. I had missed them terribly.

———•—•———

"Mom, Marshall's throwing up again." Lisa's wooden clogs pounded up the stairs to my bedroom. He hadn't been able to keep food down for two days. I took him to the doctor who rather perfunctorily sent us to the *practicante*, the one who gives shots. The *practicante* gave him multiple shots in both cheeks of his bottom but I didn't know what the shots were intended to do. The following morning Marshall couldn't walk and could barely drag his twelve-year-old frame along the black and white tiled floors. No one knew what was wrong, least of all the doctor and the *practicante*. I only figured it out later, after much reflection and backtracking on Marshall's activities.

From the time he was a toddler, my youngest son had always been an inventor and tinkerer. When he fell in love with fishing he began melting large lead weights on a small camping stove out in our patio. Then he poured the melted lead into smaller containers, which, when they cooled, he used as weights on his fishing pole. Marshall also used a blow-torch to make metal sculptures. He was always very careful to use a protective mask to shield his eyes and face from the glare of the flame. But he used that blowtorch to burn off all the lead paint on the parrot cage that had poisoned his baby parrot Coco. After going over all his activities it dawned on me: just like the baby parrot, Marshall had lead poisoning, either from the vapors released by the melting lead weights or the vaporized lead-based paint on the cage. Back then in Spain no one knew about the dangers of lead. Marshall didn't have any idea that he was poisoning himself. Neither did I. Getting so sick put a stop to all his creative endeavors. It possibly saved his life.

Once Marshall was fully recovered, I would sometimes drive out to Paco and Paca's *finca* with him and Lauren, on those interminably lonely Spanish Sundays. We could just slip into their family life. Paca would cut a few more slices of chorizo, a little more bread, wash a second head of lettuce in the *acequia* and add another handful or two of rice to the bubbling broth. There was always enough extra *arroz* for the three of us. We were always welcomed with big smiles, just like family.

Marshall would join Paco in the fields, helping load the crates with tomatoes, and Lauren would play with Paco's young nieces while I sat and talked with Paca, keeping her company, or wandered down to the river that ran cool and clear past the bottom of their fields. I would watch the small trout darting about in the shadows or pick a fistful of the large red poppies that grew wild along the banks. Seeing Paco use his hoe to change the channels, through which the *ace-quia* flowed, was like watching a choreographed ballet: he was light and quick on his feet and never let the sluicing water escape its trough. I also enjoyed peering in at the large white sow and her suckling piglets. The heat of early after-noon was heavy, and silenced the land. It was impossible to feel much but a languid ease. These hours at the *finca* were all there was for the moment.

Marshall harvesting at the finca

A few times, when I was feeling especially lonely, I would sleep there on a pile of hay under the night sky—what Loren Eiseley called "the firmament of time." Its brilliance was undiminished by ambient light from the towns and cities, since this far south there were none of any size. It was just me and the night sky and the soft snores of the sow.

In my efforts to run away from my past so long before, it was an accident that I chose Spain, but it's absolutely no accident that I ended up having to leave. What in the early years had been a simple village way of life and a place for me to make myself whole again had at the end become a dead-end where my development and education and that of my children, if we had stayed, would have been stunted. The place of opportunity, wherever that was, was not Fuengirola. Whatever our future held, I wanted to be the decision maker, not relegated to watching the world around me enjoying the boisterous good life through the glass windows on lonely Spanish Sundays.

And who could have guessed where my willingness to step off into the abyss of uncertainty would take me? Who could have known that just five short years later I would be standing in cap and gown, newly elected to Phi Beta Kappa, at the podium of Mills College in Oakland, California, as the commencement speaker for my graduating class of 1981? Most appropriate was my topic: The importance of being the architect of one's own future.

Riding a Camel

Entreat me not to leave thee, or to return from
following after thee, for wither thou goest I will go
and where thou lodgest I will lodge. Thy people
shall be my people and thy God my God.
— Ruth to Naomi 1:16

It says in Jewish law that becoming Jewish should be as difficult as riding a camel through the eye of a needle. I often had reason to ponder that as I systematically set off on my personal camel trek. After living Jewishly for years, I felt that before I could consider taking my children to Israel, I would have to formally convert to Judaism in order to feel authentic. Authenticity had become important to me. I wanted to be Jewish for me—it surely wasn't because of Malcolm—because I identified with the precept in Judaism of right action. It didn't much matter what you believed; it was more important that you acted in a moral way, consistent with Jewish values of social conscience. That's how I wanted to live and how I wanted to self-identify.

But this is where it got tricky: If Malcolm Cohen was a true Cohen, descended from the long line of Cohenim, the priests who were forbidden from marrying non-Jews, then he couldn't be married to me. Yet we had been married in a synagogue by a rabbi. So, I reasoned, I had to do research in the Jewish archives in London to determine if Malcolm's father had been a true Cohen or if immigration authorities had capriciously assigned the name when the family emigrated from Russia into Great Britain at the turn of the century. But Sylvia, my mother-in-law, was totally opposed. She feared that if I unearthed—the pun is definitely intended—that Malcolm's father was not a true Cohen, then the Jewish authorities in London could dig him up from the border of the Jewish cemetery where the Cohenim are traditionally buried, and rebury him in another spot. That was a big complication.

Complication or not, I was determined to ride that camel however far and difficult the journey. I figured I could at least try to find out the true origin of their name without going so far, if it came to that, of having his father unearthed. As surreptitiously as possible, so as not to inflame Sylvia's opposition, I proceeded to do research in the Jewish historical documents in London and made a discovery with the assistance of a Mr. Sunshine, in the office of the Chief Rabbi. Alfred Cohen, Malcolm's father, was "not shown as a Cohen on his marriage registry." Furthermore, Ronald Cohen, Malcolm's older brother, on his marriage record "shows Ronald not to be a Cohen." I didn't even mention it to Sylvia since there didn't appear to be reason to do so.

Then through our Fuengirola friend, Winifred Lownes, who gave me a letter of introduction, I was able to set up a meeting with the wife of Lord Sieff, the owner of Marks and Spencer's venerable chain of British department stores, who had considerable leverage within the Jewish Community both in London and Israel. Liz Sieff sent a car and driver to pick me up, then over an elegant lunch, listened with interest to my story. She promised to have her husband write a letter to the Chief Rabbi on my behalf. Yet, as it turned out, none of this was necessary, since the Sephardic Orthodox Rabbis in Spain and Morocco never even questioned my married surname.

While in London I saw Dr. Dan Miller for a few tune-up sessions. "So," he asserted in his characteristically blunt style, "you are running off to Israel without plans and risking another mess. You're jumping into decisions without thinking of the consequences, not guiding Lisa and not giving thought to where and how she will continue her education. As long as you have Israel. You're fearful of returning to California and to the past agonies of your marriage," he proclaimed. He was right of course about all of it, but I was still at war with the reality he pointed out. I still thought I could find my way by staying on the run.

Undeterred, I began long months of study and preparation in our common language of Spanish with the Sephardic Rabbi in Málaga. Riding that camel had indeed proved to be a tight and complicated squeeze through a tiny opening but it looked like I would make it. And no one ever raised the issue of digging up Malcolm's father, so he continues to rest in peace on the border of the hallowed Jewish cemetery in London.

MAKING *LIMONADA*

Our Last Spanish Adventure

On the gilded water of Santa Olalla, the Flamingos
with their slow, elegant movements enhance the
quiet beauty with their ebony silhouettes.
— Juan Antonio Fernández, *Doñana: Spain's Wildlife Wilderness*

A sculpture of an Iberian lynx, regally poised on a pedestal, was the first announcement that we had entered the fabled Coto de Doñana. El Coto had for centuries, as its name says, been the private hunting grounds of Spanish royalty, especially beloved by King Alfonso XIII, who voraciously hunted here throughout his twenty-nine year reign. Since 1965 these lands had been preserved and protected in perpetuity by the World Wildlife Fund. Lisa, Marshall, Lauren and I had come for an adventure. I wanted them to experience the Coto, this wild and enchanted place that had so entranced me when I had ridden through here on Favorito four years before as we headed to El Rocío. On this visit we would sleep in the majestic white fifteenth century palace—el Palacio de Doñana. We had brought along our food and would cook our meals in the grand kitchen that had once provided feasts for Europe's nobility. But best of all, we were going exploring, out on game drives with the *mayor-domo* to see the aquatic birdlife, to visit the lakes and Stone pine forests—pines that resemble a mushroom cloud over an erupting volcano—and to steep ourselves in the magic of Doñana.

Situated at the confluence of two continents, Europe and Africa, Doñana's wetlands, *las marismas,* provide an essential winter resting and refueling haven for hundreds of species of migratory birds heading to or from Africa or Siberia. It is also home to a wealth of plant species, animals, reptiles and fish, and provides safe haven for a remnant population of Europe's one native feline. It is not an overstatement to call Doñana Europe's environmental jewel.

The children and I had a fine time bouncing along in an open wagon pulled by a tractor over the sand dunes and through the eucalyptus groves. We learned that decades before, the Franco regime had begun a project to introduce the invasive, non-native Eucalyptus trees into the Coto's reserve as a scheme to produce cheap lumber. These rapidly spreading gum trees were evidence of that misguided plan. We tilted back our heads watching Imperial eagles soar the thermals, shading our eyes against the glare. Sharing our one pair of binoculars we watched thousands of coral-legged flamingos wading in *las marismas,* the tidal marshes. We saw shimmering hued bee-eaters and turquoise magpies. We lurched, swayed and giggled our way across slatted wooden walkways, high in the treetops, shushing each other to sweet silence as we gazed out into spoonbill nests stacked in an old cork oak tree. That one pair of field glasses and this experience of identifying and marveling at the beauty of the birdlife was sowing the seeds of an interest that the children and I would share into the future.

At twilight we caught glimpses of a huge wild boar sow and her piglets skittering through the underbrush. In the freshness of early morning, with the dew still pearled on the grasses, we saw herds of red deer and chose as our favorite bird the snowy white cattle egret with its yellow legs and feet. Doñana cast its considerable spell of enchantment on Marshall in particular, and enthralled me once again. I relaxed into a lighthearted mood with my children; Lisa's face softened and lost its adolescent tension.

On one of our forays a park guard came riding along on his white horse. He dismounted and began to tell our small group about the wildlife. I turned around and my absolutely fearless, nine-year-old Lauren was up in the saddle and riding this strange horse with as much ease as the guide.

We learned that the Iberian lynx, Lynx *pardinus*, the largest feline on the continent, had once been abundant in woodlands all over southern Europe. Now it had all but disappeared, except here in Doñana. If it were to go extinct, he told us, it would be the first feline species to do so since the sabertooth tigers, over 2,000 years ago. Lynx are nocturnal and very reclusive, so we would probably not see one, he added.

The Palace of Doñana is divided in two: one side used by biologists and visitors, and the other the private residence of the King or Spanish Head of State. I was fascinated to gain a glimpse of the fabled part of Doñana's history, so I asked the elderly housekeeper outside the kitchen on the King's side of the palace if I might slip in for a few minutes to see the royal rooms. Little did I know I would discover a time capsule.

Upstairs, in the main drawing room was a huge stone fireplace with this inscription chiseled in the mantel:

Creo en Dios
Amo mi Patria
Espero al Rey
I believe in God,
Love my Country
And await my King

King Alfonso XIII had fled Spain in 1931 never to return. That massive fireplace had been keeping cold vigil for him for over forty years.

Dusk descended and the musicality of the bird life was stilled; all we could hear were the sounds of snuffling and foraging in the gathering darkness. Stepping outside before sleep, into the coolness of the night, I heard the distinctive bell-clear song of the *ruiseñor*, the nightingale.

A few days of Doñana's magic and it was time to pile into our tiny white Seat 600 and head home to Fuengirola. Our battered old car, with holes in the floorboards, kept running faithfully for the entire roundtrip. As I was filling the tank at a *gasolinera* on the way home, a man nearby remarked with a mirthful smile upon his face.

"*Se nota señora que eso es un coche de categoría.* One can tell lady that that is a classy car."

"Mom, this car keeps going no matter what because it knows we love it," affirmed Marshall as I slid back into the driver's seat.

When Concha heard us pull to a stop in front of our house she pushed her face through the *rejas*, the iron grillwork over the second floor windows. We could hear her banging her tail in excitement. We were back to the reality of our lives adrift. I knew our days in Spain were numbered.

Moroccan Scarves

Be patient and have courage for there will be
better and happier news one day, if we work at it.
— Chet Huntley

On our last visit with the Bensimon family, Solomon, Lauren and I rode a bus five hours to Meknés, one of the four imperial cities of Morocco. Naphtali had arranged a meeting with the Chief Rabbi of Meknés so that Lauren and I could be officially converted to Judaism by dunking naked three times in the ritual bath, the *mikvah*.

After I completed my studies of Orthodox Judaism, the Rabbi of Málaga had arranged for my conversion with the Grand Rabbino of Tangier. But the old scoundrel, once I was seated in his shabby, book-lined office, had demanded several thousand dollars to conduct the service. So Naphtali intervened, pulled some strings and set up the conversion with the Rabbi of Meknés for the following afternoon.

It all went well. Lauren and I held our breath, dunked in and out of the tepid water three times and recited the blessing in Hebrew. The Rabbi and other witnesses, one of whom was Solomon, stood at a respectful distance watching to make certain we fulfilled the ritual, but we had our backs to them so the entire experience was quite chaste. When we were again dried and dressed I was given a formal document in Hebrew that had our pictures attached and was signed by the Rabbi affirming us as Jews.

On the return ride to Tangier, in the intimacy of a darkened bus and the privacy of ear-drum-throbbing Moroccan music, which the bus drivers love to play at full volume, Solomon blurted out a shocking revelation.

"Diana, I hate my father." His voice was ripe with repressed anger. I was stunned. "I am a prisoner of my father's orders." His frustration and hopelessness poured out. "I have no hope for the future; I will never get an education and go to school in France as the Jewish Agency has arranged for me. My father is dead-set against it and won't give his permission. I feel certain that I will grow old being a slave to my father's bidding. Diana, please help me. I have no one else."

Solomon's despair was wrenching, yet at the time there was absolutely nothing I could do to help this sweet young man of whom I had become so deeply fond. He took me into his confidence because he thought I would help him. But Solomon had no way of understanding that our family had unraveled too, and the clock was ticking inexorably towards the moment, in less than a week, when the children and I would step off a precipice into the unknown, away forever from the security and familiarity of our life in Spain. I felt sick and overwhelmed for us both.

On our return to the Bensimon apartment that night, Naphtali had instructed Coty to prepare plates of small cakes to celebrate our momentous entry into the tribe. After mint tea and cakes Coty looped her arm through mine and paraded me around to a few of the neighbors so they could offer me *mazel tov*—congratulations.

Before we said goodbye next morning, Zohar, Naphtali's elderly sister, knowing we were headed to Israel, took me aside conspiratorially and handed me two silk scarves.

"Carry them to the tombs of the Patriarchs," she said. To the tombs of Abraham, Isaac and Jacob." (What neither of us knew was that the tombs were in Hebron, in the Occupied Territories, an area of Palestinian foment, where Jews were not only unwelcome but in some physical danger.)

"Place the scarves on their tombs and say a prayer for me, for my brother Naphtali, and for our ancestors," she instructed. I carefully folded the scarves and nodded my assent.

"I'll do that for you," I promised her. Once again Zohar lit a candle, setting it afloat on a shallow saucer of water, and leaned in to read the faint rainbow that began to spread on the surface.

"Remember, God will be your guide on a long and difficult journey," she whispered. As it turns out both families were going to need all the prayers and guidance that the universe could provide.

I was in a daze from all that I had experienced and learned on this momentous trip, and the enormity of what lay ahead. Coty and I exchanged kisses on both cheeks, and Lauren and I hugged and kissed both Josef and Tamo. I could see tears glistening in Tamo's eyes, so I assured her that we would probably see her with her mother in Israel.

Solomon walked with us down to the ferry. We each hugged him goodbye, promised to write from Israel, and Lauren and I climbed the gangplank, made our way slowly past the Moroccan immigration officers, and out of the Bensimon's lives.

MAKING *LIMONADA*

Goodbye Fuengirola, Adiós España

I shall be telling this with a sigh
Somewhere ages and ages hence: Two roads
diverged in a wood, and I—
I took the one less traveled by,
And that has made all the difference..
                    — Robert Frost, *The Road Not Taken*

T he day our ship was to sail from Málaga came all
too quickly. It didn't help that on our return from
Tangier, I had a high fever and spent two days sleeping in Lisa's bed, so sick that I couldn't even make it upstairs.

Two days later I had no choice but to force myself up and
into action, drive Concha out to Paco and Paca's *finca,* and
set to work packing our suitcases and going through the last
piles of odds and ends scattered throughout our now eviscerated old house. Over the last months I'd held patio sales of
our furniture and seen Pepe's clay pots carried away cradled in
strangers' arms. All the treasures I had collected in Morocco,
the vivid blue and green Spanish pottery from Granada, the
coffee *pucheros* thrown on Pepe's wheel that had hung on

hooks over our kitchen fireplace, and all the books on the shelves—were now gone. The walls were bare of pictures and what remained were shadowy outlines of what had once been where. A circle in the hallway marked the spot where Pepe's clay fish trumpet had hung for years. The house was now filled only with echoes of the full life we had led within her walls; I could palpably feel the house's sadness but in truth I was just feeling my own.

I'd hung notices on bulletin boards at La Cepa and outside the central *mercado* announcing that our Seat 600 was for sale. A young Spaniard was happy to buy our little car, despite the hole in its floorboard, since I didn't ask a lot of money and he didn't seem to have a lot. I also found someone who had a lemon yellow VW Beetle for sale without papers; it had no registration and was in effect a car without a country. That was fine with me since we would soon be a family without a country. I realized I was assuming a risk taking the car out of Spain, into Italy, out of Italy again and into Israel. But the price was right and I was willing to take a chance.

I purchased tickets on a car-ferry that left Málaga and sailed to Livorno, Italy. We would disembark, then drive across Italy to Venice where the children and I would spend a few days exploring. Then we would re-board another ship bound for Haifa, Israel. The travel agent with whom I booked these tickets assured me that during the summer months these ships were full of students who would be traveling dirt cheap like we would do, using sleeping bags to sleep on deck or in lounge chairs in a large communal sleeping room. We were young and that seemed like something we could all manage, so those were the tickets I booked.

I had arranged that a Spanish woman with two teenaged daughters, who ran a dry cleaning business in Fuengirola, would sub-let the house in my absence. Lisa would still have her bedroom and use of the rest of the house once she returned from Israel in the fall. On her return she would get Marshall's second baby parrot, also named Coco, back from our neighbor, La Veta, and take care of him until I could figure out how to get him back to the U.S. Lisa would also go out to Coín and collect Concha from Paco and Paca, and bring her home. We tell ourselves all kinds of stories to make the truth of our lives more bearable.

Port of Málaga: Diana Gonzalez, Zoe, Lisa, Diana, Antonio Villatoro and Lauren   Marshall Hirsch photo

Early afternoon on the day of sailing, our young friend Antonio Villatoro came to our house to help load the luggage and drive with us to Málaga's port and say goodbye.

At the dock my friend Diana Gonzalez was waiting with her baby Zoe in her arms. Someone in town had given Marshall a small German camera, complete with a light meter that would assist him in getting the right exposures. He had become very interested in photography and this was a wonderful gift in support of his creativity.

We boarded the ship and parked the Beetle down in the hold and realized that it looked as though the entire Ferrari racing team was parked in there too. Up on deck we called down our last goodbyes to our friends and waved farewell to Málaga as the ship slowly pulled away and the dark water swirled below. As Marshall leaned over the railing the light meter slipped out of his pocket and was lost in the churning waves. He burst into tears but I understood that the tears he shed were not for just this loss but for so many other losses that our departure represented. I also understood as I put my arms around him and gazed into the sadness in Lauren and Lisa's eyes, that Marshall's tears were the tears we all had bottled up inside us. Thinking I could raise our spirits with a good dinner, I bought tickets for the nicest and most expensive restaurant on the ship but none of us had a shred of appetite and the food sat on the plates uneaten.

It wasn't until we disembarked in Livorno, or rather tried to disembark in Livorno, that our collective mood lightened. The Ferrari racing team roared off the ship in glorious form, those giant engines purring at deafening levels. Then I followed in our little VW driving down the ramp and onto Italian soil. "Not so fast," said the customs agent holding up his hand and motioning us to a stop. As it turned out they didn't care a wit about the registration or the lack of it. What they must have cared about was the large number of Moroccan stamps in our passports. Drug runners surely. A mother, her three children, a bunch of luggage and an old car. Perfect M.O. They proceeded to tear the car apart: off came the insides of the door panels, into the fuel tank went wires and probes, out came the spare tire and the back seat. Finding nothing they dumped the contents of our suitcases. Then, when they finally had exhausted all possibilities for uncovering clandestine contraband, they most graciously stuffed and piled everything back in the cases helter skelter, and jammed them shut. What a mess; what a welcome to Italy.

Seeing Venice for the first time through the innocence of children's eyes is pure delight. We reclined in a gondola poled along the narrow back waterways by a black-and-white shirted gondolier, while Marshall photographed Lisa, Lauren and me from a bridge above. We rode the *vaporettos* back and forth from the island where we had a big room in a beautiful old house, now a hotel. We ate leisurely meals at sidewalk cafes along the canals: all kinds of pasta and mother-of-pearl shelled razor clams in white wine and garlic. And I drank the wine of the Veneto, and gave the children little tastes in glasses filled with sparkling water. We strolled through St. Mark's Square, fed the pigeons on scraps of bread left over from lunch, and explored narrow lanes and bridges over the canals. Warm breezes off the Adriatic caressed our bare shoulders, reflections of the terracotta *palazzos* shimmered brightly on the dark water and all seemed right with the world. To see Venice with your children is to fall in love with them and with the city forever.

———•◦•———

The air in Venice's harbor smelled like burnt coffee, thick and heavy with diesel fumes. Stuck, we were stuck on the ship for forty-eight hours when we were to have sailed for Haifa the afternoon before at five o'clock. A young man with reddish blond hair who seemed to know his way around took us under his wing. It appeared he had some official capacity but I couldn't tell exactly what. He wasn't Italian; he was Israeli. He found us a cabin that hadn't been booked and arranged for us to sleep there undisturbed. It was far more comfortable than the padded chairs which necessitated sleeping upright that I had booked. The whole situation was puzzling. I never did find out what caused the delay in the sailing

The ship was full of students and young backpackers, many from Germany. Yet we spent a lot of time over that forty-eight hours talking to the young ginger-haired Israeli. He had such an air of confident strength that I was drawn to him like I'd been magnetized. Then suddenly, just before we sailed, he disappeared without even saying goodbye. As I thought about him after, I realized he might well have been a member of the Mossad, the Israeli secret service. What we didn't know was that a plane full of Israelis had been commandeered and flown by Palestinian hijackers to Idi Amin's corrupt Uganda. There was an international crisis underway and our ship, headed for Haifa, might well have been held in port for some related reason.

It was a journey of odd experiences. The ship's Italian captain took a liking to Lauren and invited all of us up to the bridge for a visit. His daughter was an Italian swim star and he was hoping she would make it onto the next Italian Olympic swim team. When the ship made its one stop on the island of Cyprus the captain invited me to go to dinner with him and the first officer at the home of the Consul General of Cyprus. I left the children to have dinner by themselves that evening as I stepped on shore dressed in high heels and a long, figure-skimming dress. A bit like Cinderella, I returned to the ship about midnight, my escorts in their be-ribboned white dress uniforms; we climbed the gangplank, I bid good-night to the captain and the first officer, and headed back to my children asleep in their lounge chairs.

As the ship moved at a crawl through the narrow Corinth Canal that links the Adriatic and the western Mediterranean with the eastern Mediterranean and the Black sea beyond, I could see the far end of the canal was splashed with ver-million paint as though red blood was spilling into the sea. "Never Forget," was painted so one could not miss it, a haunting reminder of the terrible enmity between Turkey and Cyprus when Turkish troops invaded the island in 1974.

One early morning, unable to sleep, I went up to the bridge while the sky was what Rupert Brooke called "the myriad hues that lie between darkness and darkness." The first offi-cer was on duty and I discovered that he was a scholar of Greek mythology. Standing there on the darkened helm of this great ship, the only light coming from the sonar and radar instruments sweeping ceaselessly in phosphorescent arcs, he told me a story about the Oracle of Delphi who had been consulted by a young warrior who wished to know his fate before he headed to war. He quoted her reply translating from Greek to Latin:

Ibis, redibis, non morieris in bello. Years later I would dis-cover that the Oracle's answer is enigmatic and can either mean "you will go, you will return, not die in war" or, depend-ing on where you put a comma, the answer can also be "you will go, you will return not, die in war."

The children and I were invited by the captain to come up to the bridge prior to our arrival in Haifa's historic port. About the time the Israeli bar pilot came aboard, Israeli divers were inspecting under and around the hull of the ship to make certain that there were no explosives attached. It was then that the captain told us about the hijacking of the Israeli plane and the dangerous but successful Entebbe raid to free the Israeli hostages.

We arrived safely in port, shook hands and said our thank-yous to the captain and his officer, gathered our luggage, stowed it in the car, drove off the ship and into Israel.

Tombs of the Patriarchs

Sarah died in Kiriath arba—now Hebron—in the land of Canaan; and Abraham proceeded to mourn for Sarah and to bewail her.

— Genesis 23:2-4

A few weeks after we arrived in Israel, the children and I, along with Ann's cousin, Bob Cohn, dutifully drove in our little yellow VW to Hebron, and blundered rather mindlessly into the West Bank. This is the second holiest site to Jews after the Temple Mount in Jerusalem and dates back to Biblical times 3,700 years ago. It is equally revered by Muslims and Christians as the burial site of our common ancestor, Abraham. It was Marshall's 13th birthday, a coming of age day for Jewish boys. One of those old photos shows Lauren with the silk scarves, one in each hand, standing at the tombs with Bob. A large sandstone arch and metal gate had been erected to prevent visitors from coming too close, but we could get close enough to carefully lay the scarves within. I murmured a prayer for all the Bensimons, including Coty and the children and especially, Solomon, and for their ancestors as Zohar had asked.

On the way back to the car we looked up and saw on the rooftops young Israeli soldiers in their khaki green uniforms peering intently down at us, Uzi rifles at the ready. They were there, we realized, to protect this sacred site, not us. But when we tried driving away, with Bob at the wheel, things got seriously dicey. Palestinian kids started pelting our car with rocks and almost instantly a whole crowd had formed around the little car and began rocking it back and forth, shouting and enraged by our presence. Bob reminded me how he gunned the motor trying to get us safely away, while I, in nervous shock at our danger, shouted at him "It's an old car and you can't drive it like that." Now we laugh at the memory. But it was one of the scariest and most dangerous times we experienced in all our months and peregrinations around the state of Israel.

———— ·•·• ————

Exploring Israel, a tiny country that one can easily drive around in short day trips, was especially important given the size of Baruch and Ann Gitlis' apartment in Herzalia. Like the way most Israelis lived, theirs was a small two bedroom, one bath flat that they shared with their young daughter, Sarah. It was now swollen by the addition of Ann's cousin, Bob, who had been staying with them for some months, sleeping on the living room couch. Then Lisa, Lauren, Marshall and I arrived and the small flat became positively bloated. The children and I slept on the living room floor in sleeping bags—Ann and Baruch seemed genuinely happy to have us—but I tried to minimize our presence by spending as much time as possible off exploring.

The four of us would often pile into our VW at dawn, and drive sleepily north towards Haifa, to Kibbutz Ma'agan

Mikhael, where we'd spend the morning bird watching, identifying the herons, egrets, plovers and iridescent bee-eaters that flocked to this kibbutz on the shores of the Mediterranean. I would carefully note in our bird book which species we'd spied through our binoculars that morning and then later have Baruch give me the Hebrew name and write that in as well.

On other excursions we'd head east and spend time walking the streets of the old city of Jerusalem, eating falafel from street vendors, and exploring the twisting alleys of Palestinian neighborhoods. One afternoon Lauren ducked into a narrow alley to lift her skirt and have a quick pee, with me standing guard.

"Mamá," she cried out, "someone pinched my bottom." She looked like she couldn't decide whether to laugh or to cry. We looked about but the bottom pincher of her plump little cheek was nowhere to be found.

Lauren and Diana in Jerusalem   Marshall Hirsch photo

It was in Jerusalem that we first tried *bira shchora*, a sweet malt non-alcoholic beer that Marshall loved. We walked to the Wailing Wall and watched the Othodox men praying and swaying. We each wrote wishes and blessings on little slips of paper and tucked them into crevices in the pale ochre Jerusalem stone wall. In the deepening dusk we walked outside the old city walls and marveled at how majestic this ancient city looked with the flood lights turning the walls a golden glow.

During one visit to Jerusalem, Ahbed, one of Ann's Palestinian merchant friends from the Old City, invited the children and me to go with him for lunch in Jerico. We climbed into a large car with an enormous leather back seat with Ahbed sitting in front next to the driver and headed for the ancient city. Passing through an Israeli checkpoint was anything but easy: the young soldiers peered suspiciously into the car and scrutinized our faces, and a long conversation ensued between the soldiers, Ahbed and the driver. But once we'd passed through into Palestinian territory I could see the two men's shoulders visibly relax. I saw too the glance they exchanged and almost in tandem, unclipped their seatbelts, signaling what I took to be their release from oppressive Israeli rules. It was such a small detail but so telling.

Ahbed took us to a restaurant in Jerico where shortly after we were seated, the table was covered with a traditional meze of small plates: glistening hummus, smokey *baba ganouche*, tiny eggplants and zucchini stuffed with savory fillings, dolmaths, olives, sesame breads, skewers of chicken and lamb. If I closed my eyes and inhaled deeply I could taste hints of a world of spices: cardamom, cinnamon, cumin, turmeric, garlic and zhug, all added with a delicate hand. When we couldn't eat any more Ahbed ordered tiny cups of Turkish coffee so thick and sweet it was like sludge, but delicious sludge. Then he took us for a drive to see Jerico's refugee camps. I took photographs through the barbed wire fencing. It seemed inhumane that entire generations of Palestinian families had been confined to these forlorn camps for years.

We shared other solemn experiences like when I took the children to Yad Vashem and we felt the horror of young lives lost as we gazed at an enormous pile of small shoes that had belonged to children who died in the Holocaust. Besides Hebron, there were other moments of sheer terror: our Beetle stopped running just before sundown on Friday night in the middle of Mea Sharim, the most Orthodox neighborhood of Jerusalem where it was forbidden to drive on the Sabbath. As I frantically worked to get the car to start an angry crowd of Orthodox men gathered menacingly around us, yelling at me in Yiddish. Fortunately the engine caught and I was able to drive away to safety just in time.

On another excursion we drove north to the Sea of Galilee and up into the Golan Heights. Through our binoculars we looked down into a Syrian village—children, goats and the occasional dog wandering about, women garbed modestly, head scarves and long skirts, walking to a central well, filling their water jars—another culture, another century. The villagers were going about their lives not realizing that they were being watched. It was there on the Golan Heights that I inadvertently drove off the road and into a field; as I began to back up and turn the car around we saw the sign: the field had not been cleared of mines.

On our first trip south we floated in the warm soup of the Dead Sea, head, feet, hands and arms lying on the surface of the water. It was a bobbing, buoyant experience like being a baby rocked in gentle arms. I tasted the water and my tongue and mouth contracted from the bitter saltiness. I spit and spit to rid myself of the taste.

That night we camped at the foot of the fortress of Masada. A small group of young Israeli soldiers joined us in our camping and they climbed with us to the top of Masada at dawn. I was impressed with the way they so carefully stooped to pick up any bit of litter and stash it in their packs. Their pride in their young country was inspiring.

From the fortress you can still see remnants of the siege of 2,000 years ago in the Roman camps outlined with rock walls far below. Juxtaposed across the Dead Sea are the hills of modern Jordan. Within Masada there were pools, and cisterns to store water; even some mosaic floor remained visible. I watched Ravens with delicate finger-like wing tips soar gracefully down the air currents, alighting on rocky points far below. I realized that all those years ago the Masada zealots may very well have watched from the same spot birds just such as these.

If you knew one Israeli, it seemed you knew the whole country for they shared a common sweetness of offering hospitality to me and my children. Elli's girlfriend, Osnat, grew up on Kibbutz Shoval in Beersheva and she invited us to visit her kibbutz and stay with her parents. At the end of World War II, Eliazar and Bluma, Osnat's parents, had spent almost a year behind barbed wire in displaced persons' camps before they finally found refuge in Israel. As we prepared for bed in their small kibbutz house, I was both honored and moved when Bluma handed me a wool blanket, telling me, "this is the blanket I carried during our flight across Europe." She also baked cookies and pastries for us, and as we bid them goodbye, Marshall told Eliazar, "You are a lucky man to be married to Bluma."

Each night back in Herzalia, just before the public channel 1 television signed off at 11 P.M., the station would offer Psuko Shel Yom, a daily scriptural reading followed by the soaring, plaintive HaTikvah, Israel's national anthem. "The Hope," based on the composer Smetena's "Moldau," expresses the yearning of a wandering people for a homeland that will endure a thousand tomorrows. The nightly tradition was intended, I think, to sooth the spirits before viewers trundled off into the arms of Morpheus. Baruch would rouse himself sleepily from the couch, switch off the TV and wish us *"laila tov, cholomot paz,* goodnight, sweet sleep," as he headed off to his own bed. I would tuck the children into their blankets, roll into mine and fall asleep with HaTikvah's minor key melody playing in my head.

MAKING *LIMONADA*

Summer In Sinai

*Whoever seeks the land of Genesis as it was on
the dawn of the fifth day of creation should go to
Sinai.*

—Unknown

Lauren, who turned nine that year, learned to drive on
the long, lonely asphalt scar that connected Tel Aviv
with Sharm-el-Sheik, at the tip of the Sinai Peninsula. Our old yellow VW Bug came to know that road so well
that it might even have driven itself. Lisa, the oldest, would
ride up front, her beautiful face pinched tight with feelings
she couldn't or wouldn't express. Lauren and Marshall would
sit in back. When my eyes felt scorched by the glare of the
desert sun, Lauren would lean over my right shoulder, take
the steering wheel in her young hands, and deftly steer us
south. There was something about the vastness of the landscape that made us fall silent the farther south we drove. The
car was quiet as we stared out the windows at the enormity of
the desert, so impersonal, so timeless.

There were advantages to not having a tent for camping: the stars were the canopy over our heads and we rose

and slept by the rhythm of the sun. In the cool mornings we explored rainbow hued side canyons, and swam and snorkeled in the Red Sea. Once a jeep with two young Israeli soldiers magically appeared from nowhere.

"*Geveret, mah poh koreh poh?* Woman, what's going on here?" they demanded. "It's hot, you could get lost, and you and your children could die of thirst," they scolded. But we pointed to our canteens hanging on our belts and I promised that we wouldn't amble up the canyon too far and risk losing our way. Shaking their heads in disapproval but somewhat mollified, they drove off in a haze of dust and left us to our explorations.

Throughout the inferno of the afternoons we rested, huddled together in the oval-shaped shade cast by our Beetle. We ate ice cream whenever we came across some desolate outpost and used pita bread as scoops for canned hummus, the mainstay of our diet. In the evenings we would lie on our blankets and watch the sun turn the mountains of Sinai shades of mauve, scarlet, and purple. I would tell the children stories to keep at bay the loneliness that settled around us like the deepening dusk. I'd make a small fire and brew Turkish coffee in a long-handled royal-blue enameled pot. That old pot, chipped but still sturdy, sits on my kitchen counter in California now, reminding me of how the coffee would foam up in consternation. I'd pull it from the fire, stir in heaping spoonfuls of sugar, then pour its thick sludge into tiny white cups. We'd blow and sip and rock back and forth over our crossed knees from our perches on the still warm sand. We lived that summer very much like the Bedouins we would sometimes see tending their goatherds, black slashes on the rocky landscape. We, too, were nomads, peregrinating around Sinai wherever the notion took us.

Lisa, Lauren and a Bedouin

In those years before tourism, the coral reefs of the Red Sea were pristine and home to some of the richest marine life in the world. Snorkeling in its rich tapestry of colorful corals—brilliant lionfish with neon bright stripes, clown fish, resplendent in gold, graceful anemones that danced with the movement of the water—was like floating in an aquarium. Gorgeous shelled creatures littered the fine ivory sands, while the children's bodies cast flickering shadows on the reefs below. I would look through my mask and see Lisa and Lauren's long hair fanned pale-gold and sunlit in the clear, warm waters. One morning we were snorkeling—totally absorbed in the wonders of the sea floor beneath us, floating in a big circle, holding hands—when suddenly we saw a massive dark shape in the distance. Unmistakably, a shark. I know we did the wrong thing by frantically scrambling to the safety of the shore. But that frightened scramble was done on pure instinct, like gazelles fleeing a predator. Fortunately that one scare couldn't rob us of the joy and mystery of the Red Sea, our playground that whole long summer.

Our fair skin turned a glorious roast-turkey gold from so many hours under the sun. To protect his head, Marshall wore a black and white *kaffiya*—the headscarf worn by Palestinian and Bedouin men that draped flowingly down to his shoulders, secured with a coiled black rope around the crown of his head. The ends of that *kaffiya* floated in the dry air as he walked. Lisa and Lauren and I wrapped our heads with gauzy cotton scarves, tucking in the ends like a turban. Months after we returned to California, I continued to wear one of those scarves, holding on to the spell cast by Sinai, unwilling to lose it so soon.

Midway through telling my story one evening I looked northeast toward Jordan and saw a huge tanker that appeared to be plowing straight toward us across the sand through a clump of mangrove trees. Its lights were blazing in the twilight and it looked as though it would shortly be upon us. Startled, I cried out and we all jumped to our feet, ready to run. Perhaps I had forgotten or didn't even realize how close we had camped to the Gulf of Aqaba, the narrow waterway at the northern end of the Red Sea. Or perhaps a sense of time and space are altered in that strange and ancient place. If it weren't all shifting sand dunes on the other side, we might even have been able to make out lights across the water in Saudi Arabia.

On our first journey into Sinai we met Sara, a ranger with Israel's Nature Reserve Authority. Sara's role in Sinai was to enforce Israel's strict laws protecting the coral reefs and the ancient archaeological sites. As one of the few employees in

Sinai, she had been invited by the Bedouins to join a celebration in honor of the circumcision of the chief's thirteen-year-old son. To be invited was a great honor for a woman, and she asked us to join her. Seizing the chance for an adventure in the desert's interior, the three children and I piled into Sara's jeep. As we drove inland, bouncing over corrugated roads, the dust swirled up in clouds around the open jeep. Sara pointed to both sides and beyond the gravel road.

"Those areas are full of unexploded land mines," she told us. "They're left over from the 1956 Sinai Campaign and the 1967 war with Egypt. We're safe as long as we stick to the road. When we stop to pee, just stay behind the jeep and don't wander off across the sand."

Darkness came quite suddenly in the desert but not before we came to Ein Hudra, a paradise of crystal pools and a lush date palm oasis. Sara, who spoke fluent Arabic, introduced the children and me to the Bedouin chief who urged us to join the men gathered around a blazing fire. The celebration supper consisted of paper-thin pita rounds, baked crisp and brown on the top of an old oil drum lid set on stones over the fire. The bread was accompanied by what looked to be chunks of boiled goat, with plenty of hair still attached, and lots of small glasses of dark strong coffee. In the darkness we could just make out figures draped in black, chanting and swaying in rhythm. The women were dancing, aloof and apart from the fire. We rolled into our blankets listening to the high-pitched trill of their tongues against the roofs of their mouths. It is a sound that expresses excitement and joy and the camaraderie of women—a magical way to fall asleep.

In those years Sinai was sparsely populated and visitors, like us, were a rarity and a curiosity. One afternoon a family of Bedouins invited us to their tent. What I remember most clearly is how carefully they used each precious drop of water. The mother, squatting on her haunches, sprinkled a few drops of moisture into each tiny white cup and wiped each clean with her index finger, before she filled it with thick, sweet coffee and served it to the men and then to us. It seemed as if the only things that moved with any speed in all that heat were the flies, and they mostly crowded around the mother's lips. Other than the flies' faint humming, the silence in their tent was so intense that it felt like even Planet Earth had stopped spinning on its axis.

Marshall had become fascinated with the way the Bedouin men baked their bread. The smoky crisp bread rounds were rolled and eaten, perhaps dipped in hummus, if such a luxury was available. If not, they ate the bread plain.

"Mom," Marshall whispered, his eyes large with excitement, "they're making bread over the fire. Can I go and watch?" The Bedouins, in their long black robes, noticed how taken he was with their bread making. They scurried around and found another oil drum lid for him, so that he could make his own bread for his family. This obviously gave them a great deal of pleasure judging by their big smiles and flashing white teeth in response to the clear delight of a thirteen-year-old. Those Bedouin would have been pleased had they known that when we left Israel, Marshall carefully carried that old drum lid on the airplane back to California.

Wanting to explore more we joined a Nature Reserve Authority trip, along with our friend Elli and his nephew, Leor, for a seven-day excursion into the interior of the desert. One of the highlights in a week of highlights was hiking up biblical Mt. Sinai and exploring the Monastery of Santa Catarina. That was when the term "charnel house" entered our lexicon. One room in the monastery contained orderly rows of skulls, their vacant eye sockets staring straight ahead into eternity. Another room was filled with femurs, all neatly stacked like kindling. The Greek Orthodox priests were shadowy figures, walking silently about in their gray cassocks. One had a stringy gray braid trailing down his back to his buttocks. On more than one of these rocky scrambles up Sinai's mountains, I would look about for Lauren; I could always spot her long, colt-like legs, way up ahead on the trail, as she chatted away in a mixture of Hebrew and English with our Israeli guide.

During those months the storks were migrating from Europe; many would drop exhausted at the Nature Reserve station at Ras Mohammed, at the very tip of the Sinai Peninsula. I recall the clattering of their long beaks, although if from fear or habit, we didn't know. The children and I felt so sad and helpless at not being able to aid them on their long journey to wherever it was they were headed. Our little group of four was a bit like those storks; we'd left our home in Spain and were migrating to another home, yet we had landed parched and lonely on the immense drift of the Sinai desert.

Sinai was a desolate place for a seventeen year old. Lisa was often moody and silent and I didn't know how to reach her. I think that the oldest child of any family has it rough, but it was particularly rough for her as I stumbled along learning how to parent a teenager when I was still growing up myself. I was angry at her misery and didn't understand it. I was also dimly aware of feelings of jealousy of her youth, her freedom and her developing loveliness. She must have felt so forlorn in that arid and ancient place. At least back in Tel Aviv and Jerusalem there were young men her age, youngsters already doing their military service who carried rifles slung over their shoulders. These young men were eager to be friends and show off their country. The remarkable thing was that they were eager to be friends with our whole family, mom, little sister and younger brother as well as the seventeen-year-old beauty. But Sinai, for all its enchantment, was empty and lonely for Lisa, so far from all the friends she had left behind in Spain. I'm certain we all suffered from a sense of dislocation. After so many years living in a small Spanish town, I had dismantled our life and yanked us out by our roots. And perhaps this sojourn to Israel and the summer wandering in Sinai was my way of delaying the inevitable return to the U.S. Only Lisa would return to Spain, alone, to finish her A-Levels at St. Anthony's College.

Did I not understand how much it had cost my children to follow their mother to this country that they had only heard about from my stories? What an act of love it must have been for Marshall, just thirteen, to follow me only on my word, leaving behind his turtles and most of all his beloved baby parrot Coco, not knowing if he would ever see him again. Didn't I see that my meanderings were less an adventure than, what, an avoidance? Of what, the end of a beloved era? A return to a country and a way of life that I ran away from years before? However, being in Sinai, despite my daughter's unhappiness, required keeping my wits about me and being inventive. There was time to feel the loneliness yet there was no chance to think about the future. Each day was all there was.

For a few days we were joined by two brothers from Iraq, whose family home was in Ramlah; they spoke Arabic and translated with the Bedouins who wandered by curious about the blond woman and her children. It helped to break the cycle of intense loneliness to have the brothers and a few

Bedouins squatting in a circle drinking Turkish coffee and talking about Sinai and their lives.

Marshall, our Iraqi friend and a visiting Bedouin

On our last trip into Sinai, we met up with our friends from Tel Aviv, Elli and Osnat. Together we caravanned around to the west side of the tip of Sinai where we could look across at the oil stations in Egypt, their giant flames licking the oil-laden air. Elli had heard of a spot—El Tur, known for its deep pool of hot mineral water. We all sat in that pool looking out at the lights of Egypt until the mosquitoes drove us to take cover in our blankets. That was the spot where our VW Bug got stuck in the sand and it was "dig out or perish".

On this last trip heading back to Tel Aviv, we drove until it was well after dark. Because of the inky darkness I missed the kibbutz where Elli and Osnat had suggested we all spend the night. Instead, I kept right on driving until I couldn't drive any longer. Finally I pulled the car to the side of the road, and the three children and I grabbed our blankets and slid down an incline to sleep along the edge of a lake, which we had seen many times on our drives past. The lake is memorable as there is an island, Toran Island, in the center with what is thought to be a Crusader castle on its peak. There we dropped into exhausted sleep having no notion of the shock that would await us in the morning.

While we slept our car was robbed. Picked absolutely clean. Whoever it was even took Marshall's dirty socks. Cameras, undeveloped film, money, clothes, and our passports—all gone. Fortunately I had taken the car key with me when we hastened off to sleep, otherwise we would have been stranded and in serious danger in the desert heat.

Ever tried replacing passports when you haven't a shred of identification to prove you are who you say you are? In the Middle East? The situation was especially difficult because Lisa had a flight back to Spain three days later and one of those days was an Israeli holiday when the whole country shuts down. And, like so much icing on the cake, I slipped on the slick marble floors of the U.S. Embassy in Tel Aviv when they opened it especially for us the afternoon before her flight. Not only did they have this rag-tag, sun burnt mother and her three children, none of whom had a shred of identification, there was the mother, knocked for a loop, lying in the middle of their polished floors. Never, in all our adventures over all the years, have I literally been knocked down so painfully. That shocking collision with the marble floors was a mirror image of the shocking assault of the robbery. And what did I do? I did what I've always done when life handed me a lemon. I picked myself up and moved on. But this time I pivoted like a compass back to where I had come from. Weary and temporarily chastened, I turned toward California as my ineluctable destiny and willed myself to think of it as just another adventure.

MAKING *LIMONADA*

Lessons In Friendship

There are stars up above so far away that we only see their light long, long after the star itself is gone. And so it is with the people we have loved...
— Hannah Senesch

L ike partners in an arranged marriage, Carmela and I grew to love and trust each other as the years passed, especially in these last twenty years since Pepe's death. Faithfully I have come each spring to spend a week with her, and most years I've come in the fall as well. In these last years I've noticed how the skin underneath her upper arms has drooped and both her lower legs are constantly swollen purple and blue due to poor circulation and the rigors of seven children. She's a good walker with a lot of stamina but her pace is leisurely, the pace of southern Spain. She still cooks paella that makes me wilt with pleasure, and she has retained her skillful touch with everything else that comes out of her tiny kitchen. I still stand at her elbow taking notes and photographs and asking a dozen questions about the sequence of additions to the paella and how long to cook the rice. Fourteen minutes. Patiently she tells me again and again, always reminding me that at the end the rice has to *"reposé,"* it has to rest, covered and off the heat. Carmela is categorical regarding the rice: after it cooks it must rest. She also refuses to make or eat paella for dinner. Despite being urged to do so by her daughters and daughter-in-law, she holds firmly to the old traditions of Andalucía: you don't cook or eat paella except for lunch.

In these intervening years I have come to deeply admire my Rock of Gibraltar friend, so staunch and sturdy, with her droll sense of humor and quick quips, never losing a beat in nailing the absurd. I've come to look back on my two old friends and see them with greater clarity: Pepe the artistic charmer and Carmela the rock solid foundation on which their entire family of seven children, six girls and one boy, depended. I've come to appreciate that Carmela figured out how to cook those amazing meals, something different and delicious each day, on little money. She shoehorned her entire family, including her mother, who lived with them until she died, into their tiny fisherman's cottage. If Carmela ever complained in those old days, I never heard her. It was just not in her nature.

One spring morning she met me in the plaza after she'd attended Sunday mass and took me to breakfast to a café filled with Spaniards. Amid the din of three generations of Spanish families breakfasting together, we had our *café con leche* in tall glasses, ate crusty grilled bread rubbed with garlic and sweetened with fresh grated tomato, slathered with olive oil and sprinkled with salt. For a delicious moment I felt a part of the town again—like a beloved member of Carmela's family—instead of a foreign visitor. Sitting there among the aging *señoras* of Fuengirola in their sturdy shoes and sensible cardigan sweaters, my friend Carmela, with her stylishly cut auburn hair, silk blouse and gold earrings, was the picture of money, ease and health. The years when she and her mother used to sell shellfish on a damp burlap sack in front of the morning market seemed a lifetime ago.

The two friends   Jerry Robinson photo

For the first time in all these years I asked her about her life and what it was like growing up in the decades following the Spanish Civil War. As we sat sipping our *café*, with all the time in the world, she told me about her father who just kept walking toward the French frontier after Málaga fell to Franco's Nationalists, in the spring of 1937.

"My father was a waiter in a *gran cafétería* on Calle Larios, Málaga's main street," she said. "He read the newspaper aloud to the customers since there was so much illiteracy at the time. There he made friends with men who worked for the Republican government in Málaga's city hall. Just knowing those men made him fearful that one of the Falangist death squads would come in the dark of night, and take him out for '*un paseo,*' a stroll to eternity. My father wasn't connected to city hall at all. He wasn't political. My mother was pregnant with me, but she caught rides all the way to the French border searching for him. She gave up when I was born. All alone and far from home, she carried me back to Fuengirola where she'd left my two brothers.

"*Hola Conchi, ¿que tal?*" Carmela nodded a greeting at a portly *señora* who came in with her granddaughters. "My father never returned to live with us, although when we were a little older he risked coming back a few times to visit. It still wasn't safe. He told us how the French turned their rifles on the desperate Spanish refugees, forcing men, women and children into barbed wire encampments in the sand, without food, water or shelter from the scorching sun and scouring winds."

She paused to break off a piece of toasted bread and spoon fresh grated tomato on top. After taking a bite and then a sip of coffee, she continued. "Of course this was years later, but my father's memories were vivid. He described how hundreds of people died every day from the dysentery that ravaged the concentration camps. After Franco declared victory, at gunpoint the French ordered the refugees back across the border to what my father knew would be certain death at the hands of Franco's Nationalists. He managed to slip away and went into hiding and eventually found work with French farmers who needed his labor. My father lost everything: his family, his children, and we lost him." She paused as she surveyed my empty glass.

"Diana, *¿más café quieres?*" she asked, as she signaled the waiter.

After the waiter brought two fresh glasses of espresso and filled them to the brim with hot milk, she tapped the small envelope of sugar against the saucer, pouring a stream of sweetness into her glass.

"Life was hard in those years," she admitted "With the little money my mother had, she became a *recovera*. She'd leave before sunrise to walk out into the countryside to find oranges or eggs from a farm to resell to private homes in Málaga, earning a few *pesetas* to feed our family."

"I forget your mother's name," I admitted.

"Carmen, *como la mia*, like mine."

Of course, that was the old Spanish way, but I'd never paid much attention to the details of Carmela's life, although I clearly remember her mother, always dressed in black, whitewashing the exterior of their single-story cottage.

"She lived with you until she died?"

"*Sí, sí, pero Diana, fíjate, la vida ya no es como antes. Hoy en día lo meten a una en una residencia de ancianos. ¡Y ya está!* When you get old today it's not like the old ways. Today children put you into an old people's home." At this declaration of the modern way Carmela shrugged half-heartedly to emphasize how emotionless getting rid of elderly parents is in today's Spain. It was impossible for me to believe that any of Carmela's seven children would allow her to end up like that. Besides, I remember thinking, we're going to grow into old ladyhood together, strolling arm-in-arm into our dotage.

"Everyone knew my mother had a soft heart," she continued. "She'd never turn away anyone who was hungry. She sometimes gave away the last of the little money she had." Did I detect a tinge of bitterness in Carmela's laugh? I certainly knew what it felt like to have had so little as a child and resent having your mother be so quick to help others.

"She'd walk to Marbella, down the coast toward Gibraltar, or all the way to Málaga, searching for food or anything she could barter for food. Even though the train ran from Fuengirola to Málaga, my mother couldn't afford to buy a ticket, so she had to walk or beg a ride on one of the old trucks that went by. Often she wouldn't return until late at night. She left my brothers and me with a couple that shared our few rooms. The town wasn't much of a town in those days—a small cluster of fisherman's cottages and not much else. Most everyone was poor, except for one or two wealthy families, like the *familia* Fernández, who still own the mill and the bakery on the main street. My mother was serious and didn't talk much, not like me. I never stop talking not even in the shower." Carmela's droll, self-deprecating humor was one of her most endearing qualities.

"Show me the street where you lived as a girl," I suggested as we strolled back to her apartment. It's paved and built up now in these years of tourism and prosperity, but I'm glad I asked to have a look. I've known this town since I was a young woman and it doesn't take much imagination for me to see the tiny, one-story *casita* where Carmela grew up. And that's the day I began to understand that our lives had been more alike than I would have guessed. We were both raised without fathers by mothers with little money and no status— women who had no choice but to be strong and resourceful, just like the daughters they raised and the granddaughters their daughters raised.

Late afternoons we'd always sit in the plaza in the slanting evening sunlight, people watching, having an aperitif or *un café* and continuing our conversations. "Did you ever wonder what you might have done in your life if you hadn't married so young and become a mother?" I asked. "Did you ever dream about how your life might have been different?" She looked at me with incomprehension. "I never once thought about it." There was a tone of impatience in her voice as though that was the stupidest question.

Carmela at sixteen

Carmela was so smart that I imagine she could have done just about anything, been anything. But she had to leave

school at an early age to go to work—in those years an education was unavailable to a poor village girl in *Andalucía*. Yet I, who had always fought the domestic cocoon of too-early marriage and motherhood, envied Carmela her complete satisfaction with life. She never wasted time imagining what might have been; she just relished the day-to-day existence of loving the man she married and all the children God brought into their lives. We almost never mentioned Pepe, except obliquely. She told me she had been depressed for quite a time after he died. I always wanted to ask her if she'd take me to the cemetery so I could pay my respects, but always figured it was better to let that part of our past lie undisturbed.

In addition to our long talks over coffee, we also did a bit of *escaparate* window shopping together, a very Spanish custom of strolling arm-in-arm peering in all the store windows at the pretty things—the shoes, the clothes, and especially the jewelry. Carmela clearly had an eye for beautiful jewelry. She always wore a thick gold necklace with small diamonds, and she wore the same brand of Swiss watch that I wear. If my own level of pleasure in her company was any measure, we always had one fine time together.

Carmela still didn't pull her punches. Once she saw me carefully folding up a wad of tissues from a big box to tuck in my purse and tend to my drippy nose, she barked:

"Diana, *eso es muy feo*. That's ugly!" and handed me little cellophane wrapped packages instead. But for someone who dislikes being told what to do, I heard her "*muy feo*" as caring. It's difficult to explain my pleasure at discovering how wonderful my old friend was, or how much love and affection there was between us after all those years.

After she recovered from the shock of Pepe's sudden death to a heart attack, Carmela got on with her life. She took tapestry and flamenco dance classes each week. I used to love accompanying her to her flamenco classes; of all the men and women dancing, I thought Carmela's was the most erect carriage and her's the most expressive hands. For a woman who bore seven children she was still shapely and had a wonderful sense of vanity. But then Carmela was Spanish and Spanish women don't ever forsake their vanity. She also walked every day, went to the gym, and cared for whichever of her sixteen grandchildren needed looking after. When the grandchildren called her "*abuela*" I could hear the heartfelt love in their voices. To my eyes Carmela symbolized a post-Franco Spain. Once a backward, unsophisticated, even xenophobic country, Spain was isolated from the world at large for much of the twentieth century. Now Spain has made *la transición*, as Spaniards call it, the transition to democracy and modernity in the most graceful of transformations. Just like Carmela.

During our visits together Carmela treated me with more love, affection and generosity than I think I deserve. She so obviously relished those visits that she gave up her bedroom with all its comforting religious paraphernalia—I would always have to gently move aside the baby Jesus in his manger to make room for my alarm clock, and reposition a Virgin or two and the photographs of her daughters in their first communion finery, to put down my book—while she slept in her tiny sewing room.

Every morning she prepared espresso with hot milk as only the Spaniards can make it. She grilled bread and grated fresh tomato for our toast and set the table elegantly with a white embroidered cloth so that the two old friends could take their breakfast in style. For lunch at two o'clock, she was always certain to make the dishes that I loved: fava beans with *jamon serrano*, and paella, at least twice. Some of her daughters, Rebecca, MariCarmen and Celia and my godson, José Antonio and his wife Rosa, would make us late night suppers and her son-in-law, Paco, would always organize a special dinner on my last night. Then, well after midnight, sitting together in our robes and slippers with her swollen legs elevated on a chair, Carmela and I would amble through albums of her travel photographs. There were snapshots of her in front of St. Peter's in Rome, on the Acropolis in Athens, and smiling in Scandinavia. She traveled all over the world in the years following Pepe's death.

Carmela making paella

Invariably on the afternoons before I'd catch my early morning flight home to California, Carmela would take a number and stand patiently in a line at *supermercado* Cayetano and buy a kilo of *lomo de cerdo*, a half-kilo of *jamon serrano* and a big hunk of aged *manchego* cheese as culinary treats for my husband, Jerry. I know Carmela was happy that I shared a wonderful life with him. I also know she was proud of me, proud that I read books and knew a lot about health and botany and that I was a writer, writing the stories of her family, her history.

Paco Verdun, MariCarmen, Elena, Francisco and Carmela

Did either of us stop to think for even a moment that the sand in the hourglass was running low? I know that I took for granted that this sweetness of Carmela in my life would never end. I was so sure she would come to San Francisco that I imagined all the details: Jerry and I would receive Carmela like a queen. We'd take her to Yosemite, and for a walk in Muir Woods. We'd stroll through the botanical garden and I'd drive her to the top of Broadway and Divisadero. There we would literally hang at the top of that steep hill that drops away to the blue of San Francisco Bay and Alcatraz beyond. Carmela would inhale deeply in surprise at the precipitous heights and steep drops of this city and we would laugh together, feel the wind in our hair and be two dear friends putting down more layers of memories. But it was not to be.

Epilogue I

The Bensimon Family

In the spring of 1978, when we were again living in California, I received an anguished letter from Solomon Bensimon telling me that his father had been arrested and thrown into jail, and that they needed money badly. I put together $300 and sent it in a cashiers check but he soon called to say that the money hadn't arrived and please, would I send more. At the time I had borrowed money from my children's bank accounts to pay the rent; I simply didn't have more. Within a week Solomon called again to say that his father had died in prison. There the trail ends, but the mysteries linger. Why was Naphtali sent to prison and why didn't his friend, the chief of police, come to his aid? I may never know the circumstances of his father's death, or what happened to Tamo and little Josef. I imagine that Tamo went to Israel with her mother, although we never saw them while there. I know Naphtali would not have allowed his wife to take Josef. And Solomon? The questions haunt me still. I've come to realize that just as my children and I were lovingly embraced as part of the Bensimon tribe, whatever their true story, Solomon and his family became a cherished part of mine.

Concha

When I took Concha out to Paco and Paca's finca and asked them to tie her up until Lisa returned in the fall, I didn't take any food for her nor did I give them money to buy her food. I don't know what I was thinking, but I obviously was not thinking. I don't even know if we said goodbye to her and thanked her for loving us all those years. And we drove off.

Years later Paco and Paca told me that shortly after we left Concha had pulled out of her collar and run away. I feel certain that she was running back to find us but she never made it. Out in the campo the farmers put out poisoned meat—when you drive along you can see the signs with the black skull and cross bones and the warning *veneno*. Or maybe, just maybe as Lisa says and I like to think, she met another family and used that baseball bat tail to literally beat her way into their hearts.

Pepe the Horse

I last saw Pepe the Horse on a trip back to Fuengirola with Lauren in 1986. The stables had disappeared and no trace remained. A large subdivision of Andalucian style condominiums has been built on the site. An old man walking past told me to drive out along the old *carretera de* Coín. He thought Pepe had moved the horses there. I found them but Pepe's realm was greatly diminished; he had few horses and only a small riding ring above the *gasolinera* off the old road. We met for a drink that evening and I could see the bitterness that lurked about his thin lips. He had again drunk too much and revealed to me his suppurating wound: An English nurse, Susan—another of the lost souls who had inhabited the *extranjero* community of Fuengirola—whom he had married and with whom he had a baby boy, left him and returned to England, severing any contact. Pepe had no passport, spoke no English, knew nothing of England, and had no hope of ever seeing his son again. I think he understood that he had been given a chance for family and love and had let his weakness for alcohol ruin it.

Lauren and Pepe the Horse

Paco and Paca

"*Antes de que me muera, quisiera ver a tu Juan una vez más,*" the old man with skin splotched pink and brown like a pinto pony told me. "*Una vez más.* One more time before I die I want to see your son again." It was the spring of 2006 and Paco was talking about Marshall who he always called Juan. I don't think that either Paco or Paca, or their son Francisco, understood how it was that Marshall had never come back to see them in all these years. In their own special way, as pragmatic as they were about the vagaries of life, they mourn his loss. How could I explain to them that the boy they loved grew up and left the things and people of boyhood behind?

From the sheltered table underneath the grape arbor I could hear the sounds of a freeway that had cut across the fertile farmlands of Los Llanos. When I walked down the path to where Paca used to rinse the lettuce in the *acequia*, I could see the asphalt scar and hear the steady drone of autos whizzing past. The *acequia* and the river too were now mostly dry since the source had been diverted. Paco no longer grew tomatoes, garlic and onions to sell in the big produce market in Coín. The price dropped so low from the competition of massive factory farms, he told me, that the only tomatoes and onions he grew now were for the family's table and Paca's Sunday arroz. The strangulation and scarring of Los Llanos and Paco's *finca*—the former fruit basket of the province—was emblematic of what occurred all over coastal Spain: development without planning or respect for what was intrinsically the wealth of the country. "It's just as well," he told me. "I'm getting tired." He threw back his head and laughed, but the resignation and sorrow in his voice was unmistakable.

Francisco was grown up now and had his own family. But after working hard in the contracting business on the coast all week, he headed out to the finca on Sundays to help his father in the fields. Paco and Paca had a loving daughter-in-law, Josefina, and two grandchildren, Irene, who swore like a longshoreman although she was only nine, and Javier, age five. On Sunday afternoons Josefina brought the children to the finca and they all sat down at the oilcloth-covered table under the grape arbor to Paca's *arroz*. Life for Paco and Paca was one of hard work and family. But I am certain they would tell you that it had been a good, rich life. And they were content.

Paco, spring 2006

How could I not have guessed that perhaps that afternoon with Paco in the spring of 2006, sitting under the grapes, drinking San Miguel beer, might well have been the last time? I just learned that Paco died suddenly last December, 2009, after a heart attack. When I called Paca on the telephone sobs were all she could manage. Later this year I will go to her and stay in the little house on *Calle* Albaicin, 22, and try to comfort her. I will take her arm and we will walk the back streets of the village, which in truth is no longer a village but a small city, and walk to the finca. Meanwhile I will make a book of photographs I took of them over the years and we will talk about all the good times we spent together. She told me what she told Francisco:

"When Diana hears about Paco she will be very sad." Yes, I am. "Don't tell Juan about Paco just now. Wait to tell him," she cautioned me. "Wait for a while until you are not so sad." Despite the years and distance I could hear the love she still felt for him in her voice.

Favorito

Before we sailed away from Málaga, I sold Favorito for $5,000 to a Frenchman I thought I could trust. He solemnly promised that whenever I returned to Spain, I would always be able to ride my beloved horse. And that's how I was able to part with him. Three years later I came back for the first time, walked up to the stables and when he heard my voice, his welcoming whinny rippled out of the gloomy interior. "*Hola* Favorito," I called, excited to see him again. When I phoned the Frenchman to confirm that I could ride him, he told me that he had married and that if he let me ride Favorito it would cause problems in his marriage. Like the story of Judas in the Bible, I have always thought of the money he gave me as "thirty pieces of silver." I never returned to the stables again.

Favorito, the last time I saw him.

As the years passed, I would often count Favorito's age on my fingers, wondering if he might still be alive. By the time I was finally ready to find him the trail had grown cold. The Frenchman had sold him to a Spaniard who he said had bought him for his daughter. Pepe the Horse confirmed the sale and the buyer. I sent a letter and photographs, asking for information on what had happened to the horse. Then I telephoned. But his secretary said her boss had no recollection of ever having owned him. My son David told me that I had the skills and the brains to have found him if I had really tried.

A photograph of his lovely head stares at me from the wall, here, next to my desk. The look reminds me of the nobility and dignity he personified, qualities I have tried to bring to my own life. There is now no possibility that Favorito is still alive and somehow I find that a comfort. There is no longer any chance that he stands alert in some stable waiting for the sound of my voice.

Calle José Antonio *numero* 28

Our aristocratic and cavernous old house was bulldozed into rubble five years after we left her. On the site is a four story building of apartments, all hard angles and zero charm. My long ago friend and neighbor, Patzi, sent me an article from the London *Times* that reported that the British no longer care to travel to coastal Spanish towns as they look and feel like everywhere else. The proliferation of pubs and English food has contributed to an environment that has lost all that was intrinsically Spanish. It does not surprise me.

Our Family

Lauren, Marshall and I returned to San Francisco in the fall of 1977. Lauren slipped easily into the life of Marin County. Marshall and I had a much harder time reintegrating. Marshall, who was accustomed to wearing short pants, continued to wear them but took a lot of unpleasant kidding from the other kids. He missed Coco and I know he missed the freedom of the life we had led in Spain. Becoming a competitive bicycle racer helped Marshall find his way. The summer he graduated high school, Marshall won a bronze medal as a junior in the National Cycling Championships in Ithaca, New York. Standing near the finish line and seeing him break away from the pack and win third place was one of the proudest and happiest moments of my life.

I too had a hard time adjusting to re-entry. Very soon after our return, a long time friend gave me a job in his dermatology research lab at the V.A. hospital in San Francisco. The environment of a laboratory without natural light, where there was a skull and crossbones on the door of the lab next door was as unfamiliar and as far a change from the sunlight of the Sinai Desert as one could imagine. One of my jobs was to break the necks of neonatal mice, then peel their tiny bodies and collect the translucent skin in a small pile. At lunch I would sit in the hospital cafeteria and listen to the researchers in their white lab coats talk about their projects. I puzzled that their conversations and interests seemed one-dimensional for I didn't yet understand the passion one could feel for work. I wore Israeli headscarves and long skirts, and other than the commute to the V.A., I rode my bicycle and hitchhiked for many months.

Malcolm and I struggled to find a way to put our marriage back together but despite good therapy, the stress of everyone living together in his one-bedroom apartment and the stress of trying to mend a broken relationship proved insurmountable. David, Marshall and I moved to a two-bedroom apartment nearby and Lauren, at her request, stayed with her dad. Going to college and studying philosophy, Spanish literature and marine biology was the perfect environment for me. I took some classes at College of Marin, the local community college, then transferred to Mills College on scholarship. I worked all four years, first in the lab and then in a restaurant as a waitress, and absolutely thrived. I was getting an education while my sons and daughter were getting theirs.

David graduated from high school and attended the University of California, Berkeley, studying engineering. He later transferred to Sonoma State from where he graduated. Lisa returned to California when she was twenty-one and she too struggled integrating into this culture. Going to college gave Lisa a sense of direction. She studied fashion design at FIDM in San Francisco and received her B.A. from Sonoma State University. Lauren graduated from U.C. Berkeley and returned to Spain to do a graduate program in Madrid. David, Lisa and Lauren have all gone back to Spain a number of times in the last years. I have always felt that they were still sorting out exactly where it is they belong. I believe California is now really home for them. I know it is for me, but it has taken me a lot of years to know that in my soul.

Malcolm has remained involved in the children's lives and we see each other from time to time at family gatherings. He still remains, as he wishes to be, the center of any lively discussion. I remarried sixteen years ago and my husband, Jerry, has encouraged and supported my efforts as a writer, as a volunteer at the botanical garden and in all my creative endeavors. He has been a blessing in my life and a loving friend and role model in my children's lives.

Marshall is an R.N in Santa Fe, New Mexico, Lisa is a garden designer in the Bay Area and mom to Aidan, age nine, David is a fine furniture builder in Petaluma, CA, and Lauren is mom to Alexander who is almost three. Both my daughters are the world's best moms. When they were young, my children deserved a mother who was besotted with their young selves. Knowing that, I have worked hard at becoming the most loving mother and grandmother I can be. My four children have always been my best teachers and my life is infinitely rich because of them.

Pepe and Carmela's Family

The six daughters and José Antonio are grown now and married with children of their own. In 2006, I and my two daughters, Lauren and Lisa and my grandson, Aidan, along with my husband, Jerry, traveled to Fuengirola to attend the First Communion of Carmela's grandson, Francisco, aged nine.

Carmela, José Antonio and Diana   Jerry Robinson photo

It was a truly wonderful reunion of the two families with a red carpet of hospitality. Francisco's Communion was an all day affair with delicious food and wine, a bouncy house for the younger children, all the daughters and their husbands, all the cousins and lots of dancing of Sevillanas. My husband, Jerry, had never seen anything quite like it. To be welcomed into the embrace of Pepe and Carmela's family once again was pure joy.

Isabel, Lisa and Lauren

A Tale Told by an Old Frying Pan

"See this burnt and blackened area on the bottom of this frying pan? I asked Francisco, Carmela's grandson, as we sat in our breakfast room in San Francisco finishing up our toast. "That's from your grandfather Pepe making a wood fire each morning at his pottery workshop and grilling his bread here in this pan. After his mother died and no longer carried his breakfast to the pottery, he made his own breakfast over an open fire, just as she had done for so many years."

Francisco and my grandson, Aidan, were both rubbing pieces of toast into pools of dark green Spanish olive oil as I told them this story. They both understood that this was not only a traditional Spanish breakfast but a family tradition. I described to them how Carmela always grated fresh tomato for our breakfast toast. "But they have to be good ripe tomatoes," I added.

"Yes, I know." Francisco nods vigorously, his dark eyes round and expressive. Of course he knew, since Francisco had been the beneficiary of Carmela's lovingly prepared *pan tostada* many times. Aidan not so, but he inherited the affection for this ritual from his mother, Lisa, and her childhood memories of growing up in Spain.

As they tore pieces of toast and made circles in the oil, I showed them photographs of our family during those years. Francisco pointed to Lauren at two, and asks if this was the Lauren who was Alexander's mother. Alexander is now the same age as Lauren was in the photo, the day we sailed on the *Arcadía* under the Golden Gate Bridge headed ultimately for Spain.

Francisco flew from Málaga to New York and then on to San Francisco all alone to spend two weeks with us, his California family. He was also here to improve his English. It was his first time visiting the United States and he loved it. He certainly loved the chow mein noodles that he and my husband, Jerry, ate one day after a walk through Chinatown. They ate peanuts and hotdogs at a Giant's Game and Francisco has become a Giant's fan. He devoured the Japanese gyoza that they shared after seeing *Toy Story* at a cinema in Japantown. Last night before the symphony he tried Mexican fare and as I gazed at his clean plate I guessed that he relished that too.

He's not a picky eater to be sure and he brought the same enthusiasm to all our outings, including the symphony.

"Your grandfather begged me not to take the frying pan away on my last visit to his pottery," I told him. "But I had bought it in France when we lived there, and I wanted to take it home with me. Every Sunday morning I make a fried egg with olive oil and garlic and I cook it in this pan and think of him. This pan is full of memories and I'm glad I have it." Both boys nodded their understanding as they wiped up the last smears of oil with the remaining crusts of toast. Just like Pepe so long ago, the oil glistened on Francisco's mouth and chin.

"Why did you leave Fuengirola for Israel?" Francisco asked. In just over ten days he was able to formulate this question and I was impressed. At first I didn't know what to say because I couldn't remember the answer. But after a few minutes I told him, "I lived life in those years like one continual adventure. Besides, in those years a foreigner in Spain didn't have the same access to a good university education as you would have if you were Spanish. That was important. Lisa was sixteen and Lauren was ten and it was time to think about their futures. If you come to the U.S. to live," I told him, you will be treated just like any other American, not a foreigner, but that wasn't true in Spain at the time. It's different now," I conceded.

Next year Aidan will go to spend two weeks with Francisco and his family in Fuengirola. And of course Francisco will come back to stay with us again. And that's how this family connection will continue: across the pond and across the generations. Pepe and Carmela would be very pleased.

Epilogue II

Elegy For Carmela

There is a land of the living and the land of the dead and the bridge is love, the only survival, the only meaning.
— Thornton Wilder, *The Bridge of San Luis Rey*

Carmela is lying on the couch when I arrive in early February 2009. Amid the hugs and kisses of welcome from her family it takes me a few minutes to see her in the dim flicker of the tele.

"*Mamá, aquí está* Diana," her daughter MariCarmen whispers. My friend glances my way then quickly covers her face with her hands. She starts to sob. The reality of her illness stuns me as I take in the two inches of white hair that have grown out from her scalp into the auburn that was her color of choice. Mortality has rudely elbowed vanity aside. Seeing her hair each day in the mirror as she is helped to the bathroom, she has to realize she is dying. She has to know it as surely as I now know.

Fifteen hours before, as I began my flight from San Francisco to Málaga, I worried that I wouldn't be able to hide my tears. I am a leaky kettle at my staunchest.

"She doesn't want to know she is dying," MariCarmen had warned me on the phone. So I invented an excuse that would bring me to Madrid, and being so near, I would just pop in to say hello and spend a week, as I had done countless times over the years. I will always feel deeply grateful that my godson's wife Rosa had called.

"Come Diana, soon," she had advised. But how do you say goodbye if everyone is pretending? And how do I hide my tears to avoid revealing the truth?

Earlier that afternoon, as I stepped off the plane in the Málaga Airport, the salty seep of happiness at returning "home" did not flood my eyes as it had a hundred times before. What I felt was shock at the need to come mid-winter to say goodbye. José and Rosa and their two little boys, Oscar and Eloy, were waiting for me at the exit. The boys came running toward me with outstretched arms.

Now Carmela is dying amid an explosion of family life. She is dying as she lived, surrounded by the people who love her. Two of her grandchildren, Francisco and Elena, return late afternoon for their *merienda*, their afternoon tea. Then they head off again to German and English classes. They kiss her cheeks as they pass, the TV whispers incessantly about this scandal or that atrocity. The six daughters, the doctor, nurse, and psychologist come and go, the mobiles ring, the doorbell buzzes. MariCarmen, the children's mother, clicks through, her high heels rat-a-tat-tat on the tiled floors. The table is set and meals eaten a few feet from Carmela's head. Paco, her son-in-law, asks if she wants anything, always respectfully addressing her as "Señora." Dishes and pans clink in the kitchen—the constant commotion of the ordinary life of the family with kisses, always the kisses. It is wonderful to behold. Carmela is never alone for a minute. She lies listlessly like a rag doll on the sofa, her eyes closed, seemingly oblivious to the clatter and chatter overflowing around her feet and head. It is the sound of love. This is Spanish family life at its best.

Patricia from Paraguay, a young woman hired to help with cleaning and cooking, tissues Carmela's face and gently tweezes her eyebrows. Manolito, Carmela's canary trills happily in his tiny cage hung just outside on the terraza. Eleven-year-old Francisco, one of Carmela's sixteen grandchildren, scoots about the tiny flat in her wheelchair, using his heels to propel himself back and forth. He manages to just clear the TV and the couch without banging into them. In the kitchen, MariCarmen is in the midst of preparing lunch while fending off the whines of nine-year-old Elena, who is trying to finish her poetry homework and demanding her mother's help. This apartment has a beautiful view of the languid Mediterranean four floors below, but the living space is small and always crowded with one or more of the daughters, the grandchildren from teenagers to toddlers, and me. Those gentle waves have licked this coastline ceaselessly, a metronome marking the years of our lifetimes. It will continue to do so long after Carmela and I are both gone; I find staring at its gentle ebb and flow hypnotic and comforting.

I don't quite know what to do to be of service so in between the numerous meals and *meriendas* I clean Manolito's cage, and refill his water and seed cup. This morning I carried over her orchid plants, which are just about to bloom, from her forlorn apartment to MariCarmen's so that Carmela can see the blossoms unfold. I had bought her these orchids over the years and know she is proud of how reliably she gets them to re-bloom. As I walked along the Paseo Maritimo, with the heavy terracotta pots cradled carefully in my arms, I imagined that the flowers would bring a smile to her face and remind her of our happy times together. It seems like small things are all I know to do. Sometimes I just sit quietly beside her and place my hand on her arm so she knows I am here.

Today she seems to be feeling better so I decide that I will make paella tomorrow for her lunch. If I'm ever going to get paella right, I want it to be now to prove to her that all her tutoring has paid off. I head out early next morning with my list of shellfish and vegetables. I am happily laden as I head to MariCarmen's kitchen to begin my preparations, determined to show Carmela my love. I chop and peel, crush garlic and sauté chicken and pork, make fish stock and lightly cook the fresh shrimp, just like she taught me.

"*Está muy pachucha hoy,*" MariCarmen says. Carmela is weak today, not well enough to sip more than soup, but I soldier on, making lunch for MariCarmen and Paco. Fourteen minutes exactly she always told me, then you turn off the fire and let the rice *reposé*. Proudly I bring the big pan to the table but the rice is hard like pebbles. They gamely try to eat it but my paella of love is a disaster. It's just as well Carmela doesn't have to see my defeat. Defeated by the trickery of the rice and my own hubris.

Carmela is my beloved friend but I've never told her so. After double-checking to make sure I say it right—*te quiero*—I'm going to tell her this morning, my last. When I arrive she is still in bed so I kneel by the narrow bed and put my arms around her.

"*Te quiero,*" I whisper.

"*Y yo a ti,*" she responds. And I love you too.

"Carmela, *me voy*," I say.

"*¿A dónde vas?*" her voice is the puzzlement of a hurt child.

"I have to fly home." She starts to sob while I grope for words.

"Carmela *tú eres la hermana de mi corazón*. You are the sister of my heart. People ask me where I learned hospitality and generosity and I always tell them I learned them from my friend Carmela. So much of who I am I learned from you."

"Diana, get up off the floor," she croaks, signaling me to stop this emotional nonsense. Did I tell her goodbye? I don't know because I was too fearful of using the word and splintering the pretense. But I do know I didn't cry, at least on the outside. It is only when I flee her grandson's bedroom and put my arms around Patricia that my tears flow silently while she holds my heaving shoulders.

On the drive to the airport, MariCarmen weeps, her tears dripping onto the steering wheel.

"Diana, do you know what makes me saddest?" she asks. "I won't be able to tell my mother goodbye."

"You must," I reply. "You must find a way to tell her."

As the plane lifts off from Málaga, it feels as if a stone lies heavily on my heart; an important chapter of my life is closing and I don't know what to do with my sadness. My old friend Eusebio Lahoz in Madrid told me a few days ago that, "Only a real friend travels half way across the world to say goodbye." I hadn't seen that until he pointed it out.

Yes, there can be redemption in life Carmela has taught me. Sometimes we do get a second chance to get it right. That's the gift she has given me—a gift of love, a chance to be a real friend and, buried in there somewhere, wordlessly, forgiveness.

Bibliography

Beevor, Antony, *The Battle For Spain* (Penguin Books, 2006)

Brenan, Gerald, *The Spanish Labyrinth* (Cambridge, U.K. Cambridge University Press, 1943)

Brenan, Gerald, *South From Granada: A Sojourn in Southern Spain* (New York: Kodansha America, Inc. 1957)

Carroll, Peter N., *The Odyssey of the Abraham Lincoln Brigade: Americans in the Spanish Civil War* (Stanford, California: Stanford University Press, 2003)

Cercas, Javier, *Soldados De Salamina* (Barcelona, Tusquets Editores, S.A. 2001)

Chacon, Dulce, *La Voz Dormida* (Madrid, Santillana Ediciones Generales, S.L. 2006)

Fernández, Juan Antonio, *Doñana: Spain's Wildlife Wilderness* (Sevilla, Editorial Olivo, 1975)

Fraser, Ronald, *In Hiding: The Life of Manuel Cortes* (New York: Pantheon, 1972)

Gibson, Ian, *The Death of Lorca* (Chicago: J. Philip O'Hara, Inc., 1973)

Hemingway, Ernest, *For Whom The Bell Tolls* (New York, Charles Scribner's Sons, 1940)

Hooper, John, *The New Spaniards* (Penguin Books, 1995)

Lee, Laurie, *As I Walked Out One Midsummer Morning* (Middlesex, England: Penguin Books, 1969)

Lee, Laurie, *A Rose For Winter* (Middlesex, England: Penguin Books, 1955)

Martín Ruiz, José Antonio, Breve historia de Fuengirola, (Editorial Sarriá)

Matthews, Herbert L., *Half of Spain Died: A Reappraisal of the Spanish Civil War* (New York: Charles Scribner's Sons, 1973)

Matthews, Herbert L., *The Education of A Correspondent* (Westport, Connecticut, Greenwood Press, 1970)

Mena, José María de, *Los Ultimos Bandoleros* (Editorial Almuzara, 2006)

Michener, James A., *Iberia* (Random House, Inc. 1968)

Miller, John, Editor, *Voices Against Tyranny: Writings of the Spanish Civil War on the 50th anniversary of the event* (New York, Charles Scribner's Sons, 1986)

Mora, Constancia de la, *In Place of Splendor. The Autobiography of a Spanish Woman* (New York: Harcourt, Brace, 1939)

Morris, Jan, *Spain* (Middlesex, England: Penguin Books, 1979)

Nadal, Antonio, *Guerra Civil en Málaga* (Málaga, Spain, Editorial Arguval, Segunda Edición)

Preston, Paul, *We Saw Spain Die: Foreign Correspondents In The Spanish Civil War* (New York, Skyhorse Publishing, Inc. 2009)

Rubin, Hank, *Spain's Cause Was Mine* (Southern Illinois University Press, 1997)

Thomas, Gordon and Witts, Max Morgan, *Guernica: The Crucible of World War II* (New York: Stein and Day, 1975)

Thomas, Hugh, *The Spanish Civil War* (New York: Harper & Brothers, 1961)

Tremlett, Giles, *Ghosts Of Spain* (New York, Walker & Company, 2006)

Valverde, José A, Díaz de los Reyes, A., and de Torres Faguás, Javier, *Doñana* (Sevilla, Dos Hermanas, 1979)

Vavra, Robert, *Equus: the creation of a horse* (New York, William Morrow and Company, Inc. 1977)

Vavra, Robert, *El Noble Bruto: Homenaje Al Caballo Español* (Sevilla, Editorial Olivo, S.A. 1976)

Vidal, César, *Recuerdo Mil Novecientos Treinta Y Seis…una historia oral de la Guerra Civil Española* (Madrid, Spain: Anaya & Mario Muchnik, 1996)